Moral Dilemmas

An Introduction to Christian Ethics

J. Philip Wogaman

WESTMINSTER
JOHN KNOX PRESS
LOUISVILLE · KENTUCKY

First edition
Westminster John Knox Press
Louisville, Kentucky

09 10 11 12 13 14 15 16 17 18—10 9 8 7 6 5 4 3 2 1

Book design by Drew Stevens
Cover design by Mark Abrams

Library of Congress Cataloging-in-Publication Data

Wogaman, J. Philip.
   Moral dilemmas : an introduction to Christian ethics / J. Philip Wogaman.—1st ed.
     p. cm.
   Includes index.
   ISBN 978-0-664-23316-7 (alk. paper)
   1. Christian ethics.   I. Title.
   BJ1251.W5823   2009
   170—dc22

               2008033220

Dedicated with Love to Our Grandchildren

Carolyn Martha Fado
Pinkney Susannah Wiggins
John Philip Wogaman II
Carrie Adelaide Wogaman
Paul Joseph Wogaman Jr.
Emily Margaret Wogaman
Ella Jill Wogaman
Deborah Anneliese Wogaman

Contents

Preface

I have written this in response to the need for a shorter and more accessible book on moral decision-making, suitable for study groups of thoughtful laypersons who are not scholars but who still must struggle with hard choices. I have also had in mind the college or seminary ethics classes where different viewpoints are represented by small volumes.

This is not my first book on decision-making. The first, *A Christian Method of Moral Judgment*, was published in England and the United States in 1976, with a revised second edition, *Christian Moral Judgment*, appearing in 1989. Most of my other books and shorter writings deal with moral decision-making in one way or another. This shorter book builds upon those earlier contributions and many more years of experience as a scholar and teacher in ethics. Bearing in mind that this book is an invitation to conversation, I have included as an appendix a section titled "Avoiding Pitfalls in Moral Argument." These suggestions of what to avoid appear in another of my earlier books, *Making Moral Decisions* (Nashville: Abingdon Press, 1990), and are used by permission.

I have benefited greatly from the many responses to my earlier work on moral decision-making as well as other books I have written through the years. The late Paul Ramsey once remarked that to be a teacher of ethics is to occupy an academic bench, rather than a chair. He was right. We must deal with a wide spectrum of issues and draw upon many different kinds of expertise. We cannot ourselves be experts on all of this, but we must struggle with the connections to be made between moral norms and values and the different kinds of experts who help us understand the factual world in which we live. We cannot know it all—nobody can. But the special responsibility of ethicists is to attend to the connecting points.

While I have gained much from the wisdom of others, I must take full responsibility for what is written here. I trust I will again learn from the criticisms of others, both positive and negative. I am again grateful for the thoughtful suggestions of my wife Carolyn and for the careful editorial work of Stephanie Egnotovich of Westminster John Knox Press.

Introduction

To be human is to face moral decisions. Whether we view such decisions as choosing between right and wrong or as the somewhat different contrast between good and evil, we all regularly confront moral dilemmas and uncertainties. It would be nice if we could resolve them by sheer intuition, but the moral life is not that simple. Two centuries ago, the German philosopher Immanuel Kant wrote that the only thing that is clearly and unconditionally good is the goodwill. I believe that this is true if it means that only a person who always chooses to do good can be called a good person. But here's the rub: we can *will* the good without *knowing* what it is. President Lyndon Johnson, facing difficult foreign-policy questions, once remarked to an aide that *doing* the right thing is simple; what is difficult is *knowing* what the right thing is. I'm not sure it is always easy to do good, even if we know what the good is that we ought to do. But Johnson was certainly right about how hard the knowing part can be. Even in the immediate context of family, we can love our children and want only the best for them, but often enough we're truly puzzled about what really *is* the best for them.

The highly publicized case of Terri Schiavo illustrates the point. This Florida woman suffered a heart failure in 1990, after which she failed to regain consciousness. Medical examination indicated, to the satisfaction of virtually all examiners, that she had been reduced to a persistent vegetative state from which recovery would be impossible. She was kept alive, physically, for fifteen years by feeding tubes and other forms of life support. A protracted legal battle ensued over her continuing life support. It was striking that both those who wanted to withdraw nutritional support (her husband, especially) and those who felt she should be kept alive (other family members) seemed equally concerned to do what was best for her. Who was "right"? It would be much simpler if we could say that one side was good, the other evil, but nobody can make that kind of judgment about another person's motivations with certainty. Equally sincere people often seem to differ in their assessment of what is right or good in a particular situation. There appears to be a real difference between intending the good and discerning the good. An autopsy performed after Ms. Schiavo's physical death provided evidence of the accuracy of the earlier diagnosis of persistent vegetative state. But the difference between choosing or willing the good and knowing what the good really is had gripped the national attention in this especially compelling case.

Similar things can be said about the difficulty of discerning different *degrees* of good or evil. Take the dilemmas facing the international community in the 1990s about when to intervene in the internal affairs of other countries. Were the NATO countries right to undertake military action to stop the "ethnic cleansing" in Kosovo in 1999—a campaign they carried out primarily by bombing Serbia? The genocidal ethnic cleansing by Serbians was clearly wrong. But what about the human consequences of the NATO bombing, which also killed many people? And what about the failure of the international community to intervene in Burundi and Rwanda as the Hutus killed hundreds of thousands of rival Tutsis in 1994? Acting would have entailed loss of life among the forces of the intervening countries; the failure to act meant that the genocide continued unabated. Is there such a thing as a "necessary evil" or a "lesser evil"? And if there is, how can we discern the right decisions and avoid the wrong ones? I will address such issues later.

Then there is the related question of what we are to do about the moral judgments we have made. If *knowing* the good is not the same thing as *willing* the good, it is also true that *doing* the good we know is yet a further, difficult step. Action (or wise inaction) completes the moral sequence. The well-known serenity prayer expresses this: "grant me the serenity to accept the things I cannot change, the courage to change the things I can, and the wisdom to know the difference."

This book is about making the journey, from willing the good to knowing the good, and from knowing the good to doing the good. Every morally serious person is on that journey, from early childhood. And even those who have given up on it must often live with the disquieting sense of human incompleteness and guilt that comes from ignoring or abandoning our responsibility for doing the good.

But there is a further question: What is the ultimate *basis* of the moral life? We all experience the conflicting currents of right and wrong or good and evil. But what are the implications of this universal experience? Does the moral life presuppose a deep spiritual reality? Is it religious in character? Or is it enough to think of ethics in purely philosophical or even just in sociocultural terms? Even those who do not doubt the religious roots of morality may find help from more secular sources in their own efforts to deal with moral questions. Some years ago, in another book,[1] I drew certain moral values, such as the value of individual life, the goodness of creation, and equality, out of the Christian tradition as I understand it. Some critics rightly observed that these values are not exclusively Christian—that they can, indeed, be held by people who are not committed to any religious tradition. I concede the point, and acknowledge further that many advocates of the various religious traditions make a travesty of moral life. Still, I'll pursue this very basic relationship between religion and moral life more deeply in chapter 2.

I must also acknowledge the basic limitation of this and of all books in ethics. It would be very nice if I could produce an infallible way of distinguishing between right and wrong and good and evil. That would make this a book to end all books! But don't expect that. None of us can rightly claim such wisdom. Indeed, the truth is that there are many people who have never studied ethics academically but who, nevertheless, have incredible gifts of moral discernment. And there are academic ethicists who dot the *i*'s and cross the *t*'s, but sometimes miss the main point. Ethics runs the risk of becoming little more than a way of rationalizing positions we've taken for thoroughly self-centered or irrationally biased reasons. But ethics can also be much more than that. We do well to explore whatever helpful resources we can find as we struggle to make our hard choices. Perhaps this book will prove helpful in suggesting such resources. Ideally, the best thinking in ethics not only serves individuals well in the choices they must make; it also helps clarify ethical communication among people who disagree. Remembering John Courtney Murray's dictum that genuine disagreement is a rare achievement,[2] serious thought can help us reach that point of disagreement. More, it can lead to higher levels of agreement and common purpose among people of goodwill.

While the main point of this book is moral decision-making, I also consider two related issues of great importance: (a) whether religion is essential to ethics; (b) whether motivation alone assures wise moral decisions—will a good or loving person intuitively grasp what ought to be done? Both of these issues have commanded serious attention and differing opinions among philosophers and theologians. I conclude, in the chapters that follow, that both religion and motivation are necessary but not sufficient, in addressing the difficult decisions, the "hard choices" we face.

The book will proceed as follows: In the first chapter, I will explore the difference between moral decisions that are relatively easy, requiring almost no thought, and other decisions and moral dilemmas that challenge our best thinking. In chapter 2 I argue that morality ultimately has religious roots and that our religious commitments are basic to the way we face the "hard choices." That chapter will also discuss the difference between intuition and deliberation in moral decision-making. In chapter 3 I explore the question of whether there are any "absolutes" upon which we can depend in the moral life, and how to relate the absolute to the relative. This will lead me to consider the relationship between moral values and objective facts, as well as the tension between rules and relationships and between individuals and groups in decision-making. In chapter 4, I introduce the method of moral decision-making that will frame the discussion in subsequent chapters. This method seeks to identify basic initial presumptions that can be followed with assurance unless set aside for sufficient reasons. In facing moral uncertainties, much depends upon what we give the benefit of the doubt and where we place the burden of proof. In chapter 5 I suggest a number of basic moral presumptions that should guide our thought as we face the hard choices. The burden of proof must be borne by decisions that are contrary to such presumptions. Then, in chapter 6, I take up the largely personal moral quandaries people confront, including sexual intimacy and family life, issues related to homosexuality and abortion, choice of a spouse, and the prospect of divorce. I will also discuss vocational decisions and personal political choices in this chapter. Chapter 7 will move to public-policy decisions at the local and national levels, now dealing with homosexuality and abortion as issues for public policy, rather than as purely personal decisions. In this chapter I will also consider issues related to economic justice, environmental policy, criminal justice, and the uses of military power. Since many of these issues are international in character, I will discuss in chapter 8 the hard choices now confronting the emerging global community. These are decisions that increasingly cannot be made at a purely national level but require international attention. The book will then conclude with a final chapter on decision-making in churches and other communities of faith and an appendix on moral argument.

I write as a Christian ethicist. Here and there I note the applicability of the discussion to people of other religious bodies and to persons of goodwill who do not identify themselves with any faith communities. I am convinced that the great religions have much in common and that we need to seek greater clarity in discerning both our agreements and our disagreements. I believe that the method of moral judgment explored below can advance this conversation significantly, although it is beyond the purview of this single volume to address the interfaith dialogue on moral issues as much as I would like. That dialogue among persons of different faiths is increasingly urgent in the twenty-first century.

PART 1

Starting Points

1

Some Decisions Are Easier Than Others

Some decisions are easier than others. We don't have to spend much time weighing those easy ones. Some of the moral choices between right and wrong are open and shut, even though we may have a hard time summoning the courage or disciplining ourselves to do what we know is right. But some other decisions aren't quite so easy, and we have to struggle to understand what we ought to do. Some illustrations may help to make the point.

EASY DECISIONS

Most parents know they have a serious moral responsibility to feed, clothe, and shelter their children. This is so obvious that we scarcely think about it at all—even though we may have to struggle a bit over what kinds of food to provide, how to clothe, and where to shelter them. Occasionally we read about parents who have severely neglected their children. Perhaps a child has been imprisoned in a closet or the basement and is luckily discovered, malnourished and filthy, by an outsider who tells the authorities. Authorities act immediately: The child is removed, and the parents are, at a minimum, under investigation.

The fact that we are appalled by such tragic incidents is proof of our unambiguous moral perception. The parents' behavior was simply wrong. It may have been the result of their own psychological illness, but the moral issue remains crystal clear. On the other hand, most of us feel only admiration for mothers and fathers who sacrifice their own health and well-being in order to provide for their children in the face of poverty or unusual medical circumstances. Such moral heroism, which we wonder whether we ourselves could duplicate, again makes clear that caring for one's children is an indisputable responsibility. Whether or not we're able to do it, we know that we *ought* to.

Here's another easy decision: summoning help for an injured person. In telling his parable of the Good Samaritan, Jesus invited an inquirer to see that the Samaritan's response to the injured man's need, after he has been ignored by a priest and a Levite, is so basic that it even transcends national and ethnic barriers. Occasionally we'll note a news item about bystanders who did not intervene to halt an attack on a vulnerable person or chose not to involve themselves by caring for an injured person. While our outraged reaction may not illustrate our moral superiority—for who knows what we would have done?—it does mean that we recognize the moral obligation to help an injured person. Every state reinforces this point by making it a crime to leave the scene of an accident that we have been involved in. My impression is that most people *do* act to assist injured persons, often without giving it a second thought or even thinking their behavior worthy of praise. It's an easy kind of decision to make, for most people.

We also know that it is wrong to cheat or tell lies. As I write these words, the citizens of my home city, Washington, D.C., are outraged at the actions of an official in the tax office who bilked the city of more than $31 million through an elaborate fraud. Such dishonesty, conducted on so monumental a scale, seems to defy all of the moral principles we hold dear. It is a clear case of immoral behavior, and known but uncorrected, it would sap the moral fiber of the community. But we are also morally offended by dishonesties on a smaller scale—cheating on a test to gain an unfair advantage over fellow students, or plagiarizing, or padding an expense account, or cheating on our income tax. I seriously doubt that any of us can say we have never cheated or lied about something. But I also doubt that we did it with a clear conscience, for cheating and lying are immoral decisions that run against what we know to be right and good. The philosopher Immanuel Kant, who made much of this insight, argued that it is *always* wrong to tell a lie.[3] The absoluteness of his view has challenged generations of ethicists to speak of extraordinary circumstances that can justify lying. For example, I suspect that most people would agree that it would have been justified during World War II to lie to the Gestapo to save Jewish lives, or in pre–Civil War days to lie to the authorities about the fugitive slaves one was harboring in the Underground Railroad. But whatever one may say about such extraordinary circumstances, we know that telling the truth is almost always the moral choice. It should then be easier than we make it out to be.

Of course, we must also recognize that some of the moral values and principles that are quite clear to us can also be quite wrong. I do not doubt that many of the people in the United States—especially in the South—and in South Africa were genuinely convinced that racial segregation or apartheid was morally required. Prior to the ending of apartheid in South Africa, I had a conversation with a young white South African who was as sure as he could be, morally *and theologically,* that it would be contrary to the everlasting purposes of God for the system to be changed. For him, supporting apartheid was a very easy moral decision. But to many other people at the time and to many more in retrospect, it was dehumanizing, brutal, and wrong.

Much of the world has concluded that the death penalty can no longer be supported morally, while many people in the United States are very certain that it should be maintained. Both opponents and proponents seem equally convinced, almost without further thought, that being for or against the death penalty is an easy moral decision. So the fact that a decision *seems* easy is not always a guarantee that we can depend on our feelings about it. Nevertheless, we properly remain clear about some things, and I don't need to spend much time in this book with them.

MORE DIFFICULT DECISIONS

But many, if not most, of our decisions are not so easy. The more difficult decisions are those about which people of good-will disagree and which need more constructive dialogue. An issue need not be controversial for us to agonize over making the right choices.

For example, at what point (if ever) should we choose to have the life support system of a comatose loved one disconnected? This has become an increasingly common issue, given the great advances in medical care over the past few decades, and the Terri Schiavo case brought the problem into focus. Many pastors have had to confront the question as they have sought to bring moral clarity, as well as comfort, to heartbroken families facing the decision of when to terminate life support. I can recall cases in my own pastoral experience in which the decision to disconnect life support was made under circumstances when there seemed to be no possibility that the patient would ever recover consciousness or could even survive as a physical organism without the most intensive and costly forms of maintenance. On the other hand, I remember a patient who had been given up by the medical team, and the delighted surprise we all experienced when she suddenly came back to life with her mind unimpaired. How are we to decide when to let go of a loved one? It is said that we cannot "play God," but we are reminded that in many religious traditions to be human is to be God's agents on earth!

Two of the most challenging moral issues facing American society in general, and its faith communities in particular, are abortion and homosexuality. The abortion question is especially difficult because it confronts people at two levels: the first is the choice itself to have an abortion or not, and the second is whether abortion should be made illegal. The first is a personal question of choice that is limited to a woman confronted with what she considers to be an unacceptable pregnancy and the loved ones, friends, and counselors who are in a position to advise her. The second is a public-policy issue potentially facing all of us as citizens. The two levels are not the same, but both involve ethical quandaries in a society that is far from reaching consensus. Indeed, the striking point here, as with the Schiavo case, is that partisans on both the "pro-life" and "pro-choice" sides are passionately committed. Many are absolutely sure that they are altogether right in their judgment. As a result, engaging in edifying ethical dialogue becomes extremely difficult.

The same difficulties also arise in the raging debates over homosexuality, specifically the particular issues of recognizing gay or lesbian marriages or civil unions, including gay or lesbian partners in medical insurance programs, including the abuse of homosexual persons in hate-crimes definitions, preventing prejudice against gay and lesbian couples in housing, and (in churches) including gay and lesbian persons in the ordained ministry. Again, people can believe that their positions are absolutely right and that those who disagree with them are entirely wrong. Homosexuality, like abortion, has become one of those "hot button" issues that defy consensus among people of goodwill.

Divorce, in contrast, is more readily accepted than it was two or three or four decades ago, when it could lead to social ostracism and ruined political careers. That point aside, whether to seek a divorce remains an agonizing moral decision for large numbers of troubled couples. Some find the decision easy; most do not. Usually the decision to divorce is reached in the midst of enormous pain, even when the case for divorce is relatively clear—such as a pattern of spousal abuse or repeated unfaithfulness. The relative cultural acceptance of divorce is so recent that there is very little ethical literature devoted to the questions of *when* and under *what circumstances* a divorce is the right moral choice, and how divorce should be conducted so as to minimize harm to all who are affected.

Much more attention in Christian ethics has been devoted to questions of war and peace, but, even so, people of goodwill have different opinions on the issue. The Christian pacifist tradition in the United States is long-standing, and some argue that the pacifist rejection of all war was present from the beginning of Christianity and is supported by Scripture, especially the teachings of Jesus. The other side of the debate is the "just war" tradition, which can be dated at least to Saint Augustine and may be implied at earlier points in Christian history. For centuries, there were Christians who thought warfare against the enemies of God was not only acceptable but mandatory. This was the mind-set especially of the Crusades—and, perhaps, more recently helps to explain the attitudes of many Christians toward "godless communists," with whom we were engaged in the cold war. Historical antecedents aside, the question of when and in what circumstances social violence can be encouraged remains as vexing as ever—perhaps even more so, given new forms of weaponry, genocide, and terrorism. Those who do not accept the pacifist absolute are often guided in their specific decisions by some form of the classic just-war tradition, with its carefully honed standards that define when it is morally permissible to engage in war and how war should be conducted. In practice, these standards have never been all that easy to apply, but today there are issues that the tradition does not seem to have anticipated. For example, when is it morally acceptable—or even mandatory—for nations or their representatives to intervene militarily in other countries to bring an end to human rights abuses, such as the NATO intervention in Kosovo referred to in the introduction? Indeed, how should the just-war criteria be applied in situations where an oppressed people seem driven to armed revolution?

Yet another important ethical issue facing us is the structure of the international economic order. This issue may seem very remote from actual decisions facing ordinary people. Yet all economics is deeply affected by politics, and politics is ultimately conditioned by the attitudes and values of ordinary citizens. This is true to some extent even in undemocratic countries; but it is even more the case in countries with freedom of speech and press and open elections. The moral questions get sharper as we confront the emerging competition between workers in North America and Europe and those in developing countries. If, for example, substantial majorities of Americans were to reject free-trade agreements like NAFTA, those treaties could hardly survive. While large numbers of well-intended people in wealthier countries are willing to contribute, even sacrificially, to international relief efforts, the larger questions may involve what is necessary to improve basic living standards in the poorer countries—and how world trade facilitates or impedes that.

We also face the vexing issue of immigration policy, which has claimed increasing attention early in the twenty-first century. The questions are numerous: To what extent should a nation's borders simply be open and its life and economy receptive to all? What responsibility does a society have to preserve its traditions, values, and language without which community may seem impossible? While this issue too may seem remote to average people, immigration policy is very dependent upon public opinion—and public opinion represents the individual opinions of a large number of average people.

And so it goes. These complicated issues are but a sampling from the large number of illustrations of difficult decisions any of us could name. Our problem is how to understand and deal with these issues as moral human beings.

MORAL DILEMMAS

Many, perhaps most, difficult moral decisions can be spoken of as dilemmas. We face a dilemma when we are confronted by equally attractive but mutually exclusive alternatives. Sometimes it means choosing between competing goods, when some good things must be rejected to give higher priority to more important ones. It can also mean choosing among competing evils, where our only alternative is to choose the least damaging of the bad available alternatives. We may find it possible to compromise by doing part of one and part of the other, but that is not always, and maybe not even often, the case.

Sometimes the question is one of competing goods. For instance, we have limited funds at our disposal. Which charity shall we donate to? Both seem equally compelling. For example, as a faithful member of a community of faith, I feel obligated to support it generously. But then I am also confronted by a variety of other worthy causes—perhaps sponsoring a child in a third-world orphanage or a local community recreation facility for young people, or helping the homeless or a political cause or candidate. Most of us are deluged with such invitations and requests. But not even the wealthiest people can respond to every request. Choices have to be made between institutional and charitable causes that are, on the face of it, worthy. How are we to choose?

Similar dilemmas confront policy-making by private and public institutions. Shall an educational institution concentrate on its most gifted students, on the theory that they will be able to do more good for others? Or shall it lavish more attention on the weakest students, on the theory that they represent the point of the community's greatest vulnerability? There is nothing "wrong" with devoting educational resources in either direction, but an institution or a society may have to choose between these goods. Or consider another social dilemma between competing goods: Should money be spent on further space exploration when there are so many poor people in need of those same economic resources? There's nothing wrong with space exploration and nothing wrong with helping poor people. But maybe we cannot attend to both at the same time.

Most of us ordinary people confront conflicting values all the time—how to spend our money, how to use our time, what causes to support. Even how to vote can represent a choice between good people. For some years I have been a delegate to a United Methodist conference at which bishops are to be elected. Typically, there are two or three vacancies to be filled, but there may be a dozen to fifteen candidates, most of whom would make fine bishops. It is not a matter of voting *against* anyone. But a vote for one obviously means that you cannot vote for the others. Sometimes that's the way it is in civil society as well.

But moral dilemmas can also force us to choose between greater and lesser evils. This is more difficult for morally sensitive people who want to avoid *all* evil. But we do not live in a perfect world. During the violent civil war in Liberia in the early 1990s, for example, massacres were occurring on the streets of Monrovia and elsewhere in that small west African country.[4] At the time, a U.S. amphibious ship with a thousand marines was in Liberian waters. Many concerned people in Liberia pleaded with the United States to land the marines and restore the peace, claiming that such a show of force would quickly pacify the situation. Use of military force would doubtless have entailed an evil, at least in the sense that people would likely have been killed and wounded. On the other hand, failure to use the force meant that others would be killed. The force was not used, and people continued to die. Whether a particular dilemma is a conflict between competing goods or between greater and lesser forms of evil, the moral decision-making can be exquisitely difficult.

The human tendency is to try to make the dilemma go away. One way to do this was suggested by sociologist Robert Merton. Merton noted perceptively that when we are confronted with mutually exclusive, but equally compelling, alternatives we may do one and only give the appearance of doing the other. He called this the "ritual function": We choose to act in one direction, but we ritualize or symbolize the other.[5] Thus, for instance, a church body, confronted by limited resources, may spend money to accomplish one goal while commissioning a study on its alternative or allocating only a token amount on the alternative. So while the study may appear to advance an important goal, it only symbolizes or "ritualizes" a solution. Merton's use of the word "ritual" may be an indirect caution that religious observances can be a way of avoiding substantive action. Perhaps Merton was only translating into academic language what the prophet Amos had said more colorfully three millennia earlier: "I hate, I despise your festivals, and I take no delight in your solemn assemblies. . . . But let justice roll down like waters, and righteousness like an ever-flowing stream" (Amos 5:21, 24).

Merton's idea needs to be pondered carefully, lest we slide too easily into hypocrisy. But genuine dilemmas are not so easily resolved. A strong moral case can be made for either side of a dilemma; that is what makes it so difficult.

This is the case with hard choices. They are not obvious choices. The question is whether we can *think* about them in a constructive way. The human condition does not allow for moral certainty all of the time. But can we find a way of thinking that will help us to arrive at decisions we can live with as moral beings? Ideally, that means finding ways to talk with one another more productively about the choices we face. And it also means making thoughtful decisions in such a way that we can learn from moral experience—what we did wrong as well as what we did right.

I address this more directly, beginning with chapter 3. But first, we need to consider the ultimate grounding of our spiritual existence and the values we hold. For the moral life must flow out of that ultimate grounding. One way or another, our approach to moral decision-making will usually be controlled by that deeper source of our values.

2

The Deep Basis of the Moral Life

What, then, is the ultimate basis of our moral judgments? What are the deep reasons for the choices we make? That is the question I wish to clarify in this chapter.

There can be very different reasons for deciding. The question is, what is the decisive reason, the controlling reason? One way to get at the answer to that is to ask the "why" questions. Here's a situation: Somebody offers an opinion on an ethical issue. The opinion may simply be a conclusion the person has reached. So then we ask, *why* have you reached that conclusion? Perhaps in reply the person appeals to a particular authority—a person, a group, a sacred writing. Again we ask why: *why* that authority, why that group, why that person and not some other? Ultimately we may discover the bedrock of the person's moral values. Along the way it may be that the deeper basis underlying the opinion is simply taken for granted. It may be the customs or traditions of the group with which the person is most identified, or it may be some practical consideration, or an intuition born out of previous experience.

PRACTICAL DECISION-MAKING

Sometimes we make our decisions for purely practical reasons: one approach works, while another one does not. Practicality should not be dismissed lightly as a basis for deciding the hard questions. Indeed, ethics is a *practical* discipline. Immanuel Kant even titled one of his great works on ethics the *Critique of Practical Reason*. Like Kant, many philosophers today consider ethics to be a purely rational enterprise, believing that reasonable people using their minds can arrive at satisfactory moral judgments—without appeal to religion or external authority. And like Kant, many philosophers in our time are preoccupied with what kinds of actions are practical.

That seems fair enough. Nuclear war, for instance, just isn't very practical for human civilization, regardless of religious, ethnic, and economic differences. We can all be blown up or poisoned by radioactivity. So efforts to control the spread of nuclear weaponry seem eminently practical. Similarly, it is not practical to allow disease to spread unchallenged in other countries, since bacteria and viruses do not respect national boundaries. So international efforts to eliminate killer diseases like malaria and AIDS seem practical to reasonable people, whether they are philosophers or not. Likewise, it isn't practical for a community to allow the pollution of its drinking water supplies or of the air that all must breathe, so programs to assure pure drinking water and clean air are often eminently practical. So practical considerations may be valid regardless of other differences within and between communities.

But there is a problem about what is practical: What is practical to one set of people *may not* be practical to others. To put this differently, what is a *problem* to some may not be a problem to others. As a matter of fact, what is a problem to one person can even be a *solution* to others! Racial segregation, for example, was not widely perceived as a problem among many white people in the American South or in South Africa. But for persons of color, segregation was *the* problem! The civil rights movement was a solution for persons of color; it was a problem for those who wished to maintain racial segregation. Can practicality alone provide an adequate basis for moral thought?

One twentieth-century philosopher, John Rawls, developed an intricate theory to show how reasonable people can arrive at the right judgments about practical moral problems. In his influential book *A Theory of Justice*,[6] Rawls argued that people who do not know in advance whether they will be advantaged or disadvantaged in social arrangements will want to ensure that the disadvantaged are provided for—since they may well turn out to be disadvantaged themselves. That is a provocative, insightful theory. It has been criticized, however, by those who say that for some people risk-taking is itself a stimulating value—while others are conservative enough to want to hedge all of their bets. The risk-takers may be willing to risk disadvantage in order to gain greater advantages for themselves. Of course, it is practically impossible for us to consider social arrangements without being conscious of our own social location—a point Rawls himself has acknowledged.[7]

So even this interesting theory of justice, based as it seems to be upon a kind of practical reason, still fails to answer the ultimate questions, the deeper *why* questions.

WHY ETHICS IS ULTIMATELY RELIGIOUS

I believe that such questions push us to deeper answers and that ethics is ultimately a religious or theological matter. To put this differently, all ethics finally must deal with values—what we consider to be good. And our values are linked, finally, to our conscious or unconscious belief about what is ultimately real and good. The twentieth-century theologian H. Richard Niebuhr wisely observed that our more immediate values rest upon our center of value, which is that belief about what is real and good.[8] Niebuhr wrote about three characteristic forms of value center: polytheism, henotheism, and radical monotheism.

The lowest form, *polytheism*, is an attachment to a variety of values. Here, we are attracted to different things at different times—or at the same time—and we invest each with absolute devotion at that moment. This is a religion of fads, of passing attractions, and in the end it is only self-centered.

At a higher level is *henotheism*—worship of the tribe, which can be a selfless form of valuing. We are loyal to our group (family, community, church, nation, even humanity as a whole), investing it with absolute devotion. We may even be led to give our lives for that overarching value. In the long run, however, our devotion is a passing thing, no matter how complete it may be at the time. Moreover, *henotheism* is not inclusive of all of reality. If, for example, we worship our country ("my country, right or wrong"), we have excluded the rest of humanity. One's family is not even as inclusive a value as the community or the nation. And even humanity as a whole excludes the teeming wonders of the rest of creation.

The highest loyalty, the most inclusive value, is to what Niebuhr calls *radical monotheism*, the worship of the one God, who is center and source of all being and the grounding of all other values. To say that something is good is then to say that it expresses the ultimate basis of all being, of all that is. This is the only value center that connects ethics with what is truly universal.

The importance of the center of value that controls our moral outlook may be illustrated by the value we invest in competitive events, such as a football game. For players and fans alike, the value is clear—winning the game by scoring more points than the other team. At the moment, that value can be all-consuming. We *intensely* want our team to win. Successes and failures are clearly marked. Rules of the game are laid out precisely, and infractions, when discovered by officials, are penalized. It's as though a whole ethical universe were focused, here and now, on the playing field. But does it really *matter,* in any ultimate sense? The outcome of the game, even a championship match, is of no consequence to the vast majority of the world's people. Indeed, even most of those who are caught up in the intensity of the moment will soon enough forget. In most sports, records and statistics are long remembered by the true aficionados. But not for centuries, certainly not for millennia. In the long run, it is as though the event and the records had never been.

Is that also true of our moral choices in general? There are passionately held values, and principles and rules to help one express and preserve them. They all may be taken to embody what is universally human about us. But still, do they *matter*? In the long, long run, will it be as though nothing had actually happened? Do our moral decisions have enduring consequences? Is life, taken as a whole, like the football game, passionate in intensity but destined to be forgotten? If it is, we can greatly value life as a game, elaborating principles and rules to enhance its meaning. There can even be space for devotion to great causes, for the sake of which one can be willing to sacrifice everything. Although the moral life would mean absolutely nothing *ultimately*, it can mean very much personally and socially within the limited horizon of human experience. So those of us who approach ethics from a theological standpoint, as Niebuhr has done, should be slow to dismiss the ethical commitments of those who do not.

But God cannot be dismissed so casually, either. Without God, the universe is devoid of ultimate purpose, and human life is finally to no end. That matters! The fact that it matters does not establish the reality of God; but it does mean that belief or disbelief in God is worthy of serious reflection by morally mature people.

It is beyond the scope of this book to pursue the question of God fully, but I can't end the discussion without making two points about God, science, and the universe itself.

First, while science does not and cannot finally resolve the God question, it can be helpful. Take the big bang theory. A large consensus among relevant astronomers and physicists may not guarantee its permanence as a scientific finding. But, for the moment at least, it seems to be startling evidence of how an unimaginably vast universe could begin from an unimaginably small starting point. This is close to the old theological principle of *creatio ex nihilo*—creation from nothing. But how are we to explain the beginning? If it was not an act of

God, then what was it? Scientists and knowledgeable theologians have long accepted that no God planned the contents of creation in detail. The specific composition of all organic life, up to and including human beings, is persuasively accounted for by evolution. But, to express a truism, everything that exists has *potentially* existed from the beginning. That does not mean that human life specifically as we know it was fully developed in the mind of God. It does mean, however, that built into creation from the beginning was the possibility that there could emerge conscious, valuing beings like ourselves. Perhaps there are, on myriads of other planets, beings that are much more advanced as conscious, valuing beings than we are. I hope so. But the really interesting point is that apart from there being a God, beings like ourselves are the highest point in creation. I am not quite prepared to say that the cause of this great universe is less conscious and purposive than I am. I'd rather take a leap of faith, believing in something greater than myself.

My second point follows from this. Our theory of the origin of the universe either reduces that origin to something less than human or raises it to something more. The great religions emphasize the "something more," although they often express this "more" through story and myth. This leads us to the question of revelation.

ACCEPTABLE AND UNACCEPTABLE FORMS OF REVELATION

In general, revelation can be defined as the imparting or receiving of an important but previously unknown truth. Thus religious revelation can be taken as disclosing the nature of the whole of being, something that is far beyond anybody's direct experience. Often revelation is understood to mean knowledge imparted by an authoritative or supernatural source. One bumper sticker says, "God said it. I believe it. That settles it." In this view, which in some circles is the common wisdom, religious revelation involves truth from on high, delivered in a take-it-or-leave-it form. The Bible, the Qur'an, the *Book of Mormon*, and other sacred writings were, according to this view, more or less dictated by God. Therefore, since it all came from God, everything in such a writing is absolutely true. But there are serious problems with such a view of revelation. If a writing announces that its message has come directly from God, how are we to adjudicate similar claims made by a variety of such writings? Would a Muslim accept the *Book of Mormon* as a direct message from God? Would a Mormon accept the Qur'an as such an authentic message? Would a Christian fundamentalist accept either the Qur'an or the *Book of Mormon*? Moreover, all of the sacred writings with which I am familiar contain factual claims that cannot be taken literally. Most also contain questionable moral teachings. But even though they cannot always be taken literally, sacred writings may still convey important truths. We need to remember that even myths can be deeply truthful, although they may also invite us to accept claims of factual truth that cannot be sustained: For example, the world was *not* created in six days. Flood waters never covered the whole earth. The sun did not stand still to enable an Israelite victory.

Nevertheless, while myth is often expressed in factual form, its meaning transcends its factual garments. Religious myths always need to be seen in terms of the ultimate meanings they do or do not convey. Some express the dark side of human fears—such as the story of Lot's wife turning into a pillar of salt. Others convey hope and love—such as the beautiful story of Jesus' birth in Luke. It remains for every generation of the faithful to sort through its religious legacies, be nurtured by the best it discovers, and honestly set the rest aside. Moral truths are not revealed to us in indisputable form, but deep moral truth still depends upon revelation. How can that be?

Revelation is those aspects of experience that we take to disclose the nature of the whole of being, most of which, again, is far beyond direct human experience in our limited world and our limited lifetimes.

A true revelation is one that brings everything into focus. Thus, for Christians, Jesus Christ is taken to be our best revelation of the nature of God. If, as Christians believe, the reality of God is indeed expressed through Christ, that has enormous moral implications.

THE USEFUL INCOMPLETENESS OF RELIGIOUS TRADITION

It has probably occurred to you that we do not all experience Jesus Christ in the same way. Indeed, most of us continue to discover more about Jesus the longer we live and the more we face the difficulties and possibilities of human life. In this respect, we are the inheritors of two millennia of Christian tradition, much of which is grounded in Scripture and Hebrew and Christian history. The tradition is loaded with insight; at its best, it represents the honest struggle of generations of good people to live out its implications in their personal and social existence. The scriptural forebears, the lives of saints like Francis of Assisi, the formative minds of people such as Augustine, Martin Luther, Catherine of Siena, John Calvin, and John Wesley, and the prophetic spirits of Thomas More and Martin Luther King Jr. all have much to teach us about the moral life. The great hymns of faith, many thousands of them, contain eloquent testimonies of faith by poets of successive generations.

All this *forms* us as persons and as a people of faith.

Still, tradition is imperfect and is, in some cases, a disruption of Christian moral life. It has its dark side. For example, slavery was an acceptable part of the tradition for most of the Christian centuries. Women have historically been relegated to secondary status—and still are, in much of institutional Christianity. Religious persecution, including unimaginable tortures and wholesale slaughter, is also a part of the tradition. Perhaps the best that can be said about this dark and evil side of the tradition is that it helps us better to recognize, by contrast, the true Christian moral life, just as the crucifixion of Christ illuminates both the depth of divine love and the evil of which we are all capable. But that is faint praise indeed!

Yet we cannot do without Christian tradition. It is a very rich and indispensable source of faith and life, and without it we could not be Christian. But tradition—including Scripture—cannot be relied upon to supply answers to specific moral questions without our further thought about the meaning of our faith and the relevant historical and factual context. Some of the moral teachings of the Bible, for instance, are far more insightful than others. Paul's great wisdom on the disciplines of love, in 1 Corinthians 13, is as compelling as it is eloquent. But his comments on the superiority of men over women in 1 Corinthians 11 have doubtless done more harm than good throughout Christian history.

MORAL VIRTUE AND CHARACTER

Thomas Aquinas defined virtue as a disposition of the will toward a good end. Another way to put this is that a virtue is a *habit*. Virtuous people habitually act in good ways, sometimes without even thinking about it. To a virtuous person, evildoing or self-centered behavior is simply unthinkable. If a virtuous person sees another in need, the impulse to help is almost automatic. Nobody is *totally* virtuous, of course. But a person's character is a reflection of how much her or his life is an expression of virtue. First Corinthians 13 suggests an important point: moral virtues matter. "If I have prophetic powers, and understand all mysteries and all knowledge, and if I have all faith, so as to remove mountains, but do not have love, I am nothing."

So moral virtues define our *character*. And character is the indispensable starting point for moral decision-making. As noted earlier, Immanuel Kant even argued that the only thing that is unquestionably good is the goodwill. It is true, of course, that people may do good things accidentally or while pursuing other ends, even though they do not will the good. But to be a person of goodwill is to seek the good consciously and wholeheartedly. It is to be a virtuous person.

What are the virtues that constitute Christian character? Much more has been said and written about this than we have space to recount. But for me three virtues are quite central: honesty, humility, and love. To be honest is to make a habit of truth telling and to refrain from misleading others. Recall Immanuel Kant's insistence that it is *always* wrong to tell a lie. The issue may be more complex than he understood (or he may have been unacceptably inflexible), but a disposition toward complete honesty is one of the virtues without which moral life falls short. Practically speaking, implementing the virtue may be challenging, but there is no doubt that honesty is itself a central part of moral character.

Also central to moral characer is humility, a deep sense of our limitations, a recognition that we do not know it all. Humility is built upon both the worship of the God who is greater than we are and an openness to new truth. Humility is not a retreat from convictions; it is not skepticism about every attainable truth. It is, rather, the recognition that there is always something more than we can know, especially, that God and the ways of God far transcend our human limitations. Alfred Tennyson's lines speak to the point: "Our little systems have their day, they have their day and cease to be; they are but broken lights of thee, and thou, O Lord, art more than they." Such words bespeak the virtue of humility; they caution us against intellectual pretense and religious fanaticism.

But, as important as honesty and humility are, Paul is right in that eloquent chapter 13 of 1 Corinthians in identifying love as the foundational Christian virtue. To be a loving person is to be altogether positive in one's outlook on life and to care genuinely about the well-being of others. It is to be kind and compassionate, patient with the shortcomings and failures of others, seeking to bring out the best in others. Love is the attitude formed out of grace, out of God's love for us, and with gratitude. The more grateful we are, the less resentful we can be, and the more we are filled with resentment, the less we can be filled with gratitude.

A virtuous life must be cultivated like a garden. It isn't automatic. Nurture in a loving family and by an enlightened, profound faith tradition is an important condition of the development of a virtuous life, but it is not sufficient. Most of us must work at becoming more virtuous. We grow in our appreciation of the positive influences, such as the nurturing traditions and praiseworthy relationships, even as we learn from our shortcomings and mistakes. We strive to make a good life habitual, just as musicians or athletes work to perfect their ability to perform well, almost as second nature. Even a "natural" has to work to rise to her or his potential, but since humility is a core virtue, the work of perfecting ourselves cannot lead to pride in our virtue. Rather, it can lead to gratitude to God for creating all of us with such potentialities.

INTUITION AND DELIBERATION
IN MORAL DECISION-MAKING

Moral character is a critically important foundation from which to make hard moral choices. Decisions for the good rest heavily upon the decision-maker being a person of goodwill. This is so true that situational or contextual ethical thinkers, such as Joseph Fletcher and Paul Lehmann, come close to saying that a loving person will simply do loving things and that a Christian who is really a Christian will do what a Christian does "to make human life human," as Paul Lehmann has said. Another way to put this is to say that those who are truly loving or truly Christian will make the hard choices on the basis of intuition. If I am really good, my intuitions can be depended upon as a sure guide. A truly moral person is a person of moral discernment.

That is an important part of the truth about moral decision-making. We have all known people who, though lacking in intellectual sophistication, are able to see through false values and inauthentic human behavior. They just *seem to know* what is good and right. They are not deflected from the right course by self-interest and the easy idolatries of their generation. This gift of intuition is conferred by a well-nurtured moral character.

But if it is true that such intuitive discernment is often given to people of goodwill, it may be equally true that even such people can be mistaken. A distinction has to be drawn between being good and knowing good. We can be grateful that the two so often go together. But we know that often they do not. Being good is not the same thing as being omniscient. There is so much we simply do not know. There are ramifications to decisions—even those made in good faith by people with extraordinary gifts of moral intuition—that cannot be foreseen without careful study and thought. Whether or not the old saying that "the road to hell is paved with good intentions" is true, it is at least right in reminding us that good intentions alone are often not good enough. Good intentions need thoughtful direction, even if we are not inclined to consign well-intentioned but mistaken people to hell!

In a nutshell, the moral life is made up of both heart and mind. That is evident when we see good people, even really good people, who flatly disagree about a troubling moral choice, whether it is a political or economic decision on a grand scale or a more immediate dilemma in family life or the immediate community. Good people can disagree. The fact that moral life is both heart and mind is also evident when we see good people change their minds on the basis of new experience.

In my early years as a seminary professor, I was frustrated by my inability to influence the thinking of a particularly gifted student, who was, I thought, simply wrong about a host of issues, especially about how to deal with poverty. I was troubled to see him go forth to serve as a minister. His church appointment was to a working-class town in a part of the country where labor unions are not accepted and where poor workers are badly exploited. As a pastor he saw the hurt this caused—the disease, the loss of opportunity, the struggles to make ends meet. He was honest enough to see this. Much to our surprise, a year or two later he came back to the seminary to ask how to go about organizing a labor union! There was nothing wrong with his basic character, but until he was assigned to that hard-scrabble church situation, he simply had not had enough experience. People of character can grow, but they also need to experience more and to think more in order to do it.

Intuition and thought are not necessarily opposed to each other. Later, we shall address the question of how best to do our moral thinking, but here I want to emphasize the relationship between thought and intuition. Intuition can be a very helpful, even indispensable, guide to us in many situations. Nevertheless, our intuitions in one situation can be improved greatly if we have thought problems through more carefully in previous situations. A good test of any approach to moral decision-making is whether it prepares us to make better intuitive judgments.

One might well conclude, from this chapter, that moral decisions are all relative. No matter how good we are as persons, and despite our grounding in a deep religious faith, we can be mistaken in our moral judgments. Have we slipped into a sinkhole of relativism? Are there no absolutes upon which we can depend? I turn to these questions in the next chapter.

3

The Absolute and the Relative in Moral Life

Twenty-first-century people throughout the world struggle with the question of what is absolute and what is relative in moral decision-making. In this chapter, I will deal with that question and the related question of how we are to relate moral values to objective facts. So, to begin, how does the difference between absolute and relative show up in ethical decision-making?

A pacifist considers the refusal to participate in war to be an absolute, while those persuaded by the just-war tradition take that to be a relative question. Those espousing the "pro-life" position regard abortion to be absolutely wrong, while those who are "pro-choice" consider such a decision to be relative. Many Christians and most Muslims regard abstaining from alcohol to be an absolute; others disagree. Many take it as an absolute that sexual expression should be confined to marriage. Many are convinced that sexual expression should be limited to heterosexual relationships—while others disagree with such absolutes. The debates rage. How, indeed, are we to relate the absolute to the relative?

HAVE WE BECOME TOO RELATIVISTIC?

Many conservative Christians decry what they perceive to be the growing relativism of American culture. In his provocative book *Against the Night*, Charles Colson exclaimed that "today's radical individualism . . . has changed our public ethos. No longer are we guided by virtue or tradition. . . . There is no universal truth, no absolute code of conduct; there is only truth for me and truth for you."[9] As a pastor, I would occasionally receive a letter that seemed to have been written in this spirit. One such letter said, "I am sorry that churches now have a decrease in membership if they are mainline ones, but I can understand why now when they don't stand for much of anything. We are to go by God's word and he says some things are wrong." Most religious fundamentalists— Christians and those from other faith traditions—insist, often stridently and sometimes violently, on a return to the absolutes. By this they often mean highly specific moral rules that must be followed without question. On the other hand, the opposite, more relativistic tendency is also well represented in our culture. Surprisingly, a degree of relativism apparently is expressed even by many fundamentalist or conservative Christians. A 2001 Barna Research Group study found that 54 percent of "born again" Christians believe that "moral truth depends on the situation," while only 32 percent in this group held that "moral truth is unchanging."[10] It is also true that numbers of more liberal Christians are also absolutists. The conservatives may be especially concerned about, say, homosexuality, while some liberals may be absolutist about something like animal rights. Much of the relativism in our time may reflect a reaction against what many perceive to be the suffocation of the moral absolutisms of our age.

Of course, people may be absolutists about some things and relativists about others. And, as anthropologists point out, there is little agreement among different societies as to what are the true absolutes and what should be considered relative. Does Christian ethics help us to understand this relationship between relativism and absolutism?

There are, I think, some false starts that are in need of criticism. For example, complete, full-blown ethical relativism, at least as the view that all values and moral perspectives are equally good, just won't work, because it undermines all ethics. Colson is right about that. If all opinions are equally good, then there is no universal foundation for any of them and no basis for distinguishing between good and evil or right and wrong. Thoroughgoing ethical relativism is ultimately the destruction of ethics itself.

On the other hand, there are problems with the notion that we can know moral demands with absolute certainty, having total clarity about what is right and wrong, complete certainty about good and evil, fixed ideas about what is justice and injustice. Something in our humanity craves that kind of certainty, a bedrock upon which to base our actions and guide our conscience. This need may be especially felt in face of the insecurities of the twenty-first-century world, and it is evident among some adherents of all of the great world religions. Nonetheless, something is wrong with absolutism. That is obvious with true extremists, like the Taliban of Afghanistan and the Christian Reconstructionist movement of Rousas Rushdoony and Gary North, who take Scripture literally and advocate strict conformity to biblical commandments as the foundation of public law. The Reconstructionist movement is extreme and not accepted by most Christian fundamentalists, any more than the Taliban are accepted by most Muslims. But the idea that the moral injunctions of the Bible or the Qur'an are to be taken literally as absolute commands of God is common enough.

Using sacred Scriptures as an absolute bedrock for ethics flounders for two reasons. First, the direct moral teachings are not always consistent with one another; second, even among fundamentalists some of these teachings are repugnant to their modern ethical sensibilities. For instance, I do not believe that most Christian fundamentalists would agree with Leviticus 20 that homosexuals should be put to death, nor with the very strict dietary and clothing requirements of the Holiness Code. Even some New Testament teachings, such as loving actions toward one's enemies and the condemnation of wealth, do not find much acceptance in conservative Christian circles. More liberal Christians are offended by genocidal actions and commandments in the Old Testament (as in the destruction of Jericho) and the patriarchal sentiments of 1 Corinthians 11.

One might wonder about inconsistent applications of the Ten Commandments in that regard. Even fundamentalists, who argue in favor of biblical inerrancy and could logically be expected then to follow all of the Bible's injunctions, including the Ten Commandments, find ways to rationalize exceptions to some of them—such as killing (in the case of war or capital punishment) or bearing false witness (such as slandering political candidates whose views differ from theirs).

An even deeper problem lies in the difficulty in answering the question, *why* the Bible or other sacred Scriptures should be used in a literalistic way. What is the basis for such an absolutist conception of biblical authority? It cannot be because of statements made within the Bible itself—or how could we choose between, say, the Bible and the Qur'an and the *Book of Mormon*? Even if we declare that we know the sacred Scripture to be literally true in every respect because of the witness of the Holy Spirit within us as we read its passages, then we are invoking an obviously subjective principle. Similarly, we can argue from the biblically inspired transformation of our own life and the lives of others. Commendable as that may be, skeptics can ask about negative transformations having scriptural rootage, or point out that other religions, with their own, very different scriptures, can say the same thing.

By raising these questions about scriptural literalism I do not mean to suggest that the Bible is not a primary source of ethical insight. But it is a false start to consider every aspect of the Bible to be equally important or even equally true.

Many Christians who are by no means fundamentalists prefer to say simply that the absolute basis of Christian ethics is finding and doing "the will of God." If ethics is ultimately based upon religious conviction, the will of God is obviously very central. But the question then arises, how are we to *know* the will of God? When Christians announce with certainty that something is the will of God, they may be basing this upon their own intuition or some other source of moral insight that they can impute to God. What are these other sources that their certainty is grounded upon? Again, the quest is for some objective basis or principle for discerning, with assurance, what is the will of God.

THE NATURAL-LAW APPROACH

Historically the different versions of natural law have sought to provide some degree of certainty about moral decision-making. Sometimes the principles or rules derived from natural law are treated as absolutely binding. In crude form, natural law is represented as basing our judgments upon what appears to be "natural." Thus, for instance, homosexuality is considered to be absolutely immoral because the bodily parts are clearly intended for heterosexual intercourse. To engage in homosexual practice is therefore taken to be contrary to nature.

More sophisticated versions of natural law seek to discern the moral structure of the universe, as it can be known by human reason. Such views of natural law have high confidence in the ability of the human mind to know, perhaps with certainty, what is the moral law of the universe.

The ancient Stoics had such confidence in human reason. The Stoics granted that human reason is often clouded by materialistic corruptions of one kind or another, but they remained confident of unclouded reason's direct connection with the rational mind that is at the center of all being. They believed that universal truth, in absolute form, is accessible to us and becomes the ultimate criterion upon which we can judge the civil law of states and the moral customs or thematic norms common to peoples everywhere.

A different form of natural law was developed by the great medieval thinker Thomas Aquinas, who was deeply influenced by the ethics of Aristotle. Aquinas held that all beings and objects in the natural world have an end, or *telos*, that defines their essential nature. Further, the fulfillment of each *telos* is universally and absolutely binding. This is as true of the institutions common to humanity (family, state, economic life, etc.) as it is of persons themselves. In Roman Catholic moral teaching, for centuries influenced by this tradition, the absolute appeal of natural law may be waning. But it is still reflected in much Catholic teaching, for example, in the absolute rejection of abortion and even of contraception—the latter officially rejected because it obstructs the natural *telos* of the sexual act, which is to be open to new life.

The problem, critics charge, in such absolute reliance upon natural law, in either its Stoic or its Thomist form, comes in trying to apply it. It is one thing to affirm a moral order to the universe, but it may be quite another to identify its contents. How can we *know* what is absolutely required by natural law? Natural law may appear to be a very objective basis for moral decision-making, but when we seek to express its requirements, this objectivity becomes much more subjective.

Kantian moral thought gets at the issue in another way. Kant used the term "categorical imperative" to argue that all ethics is grounded in one true absolute, and that the rationale (or "maxim") used to justify one's action could become the basis of universal law. A moral person does not, he argued, make himself or herself an exception to rules that must apply equally to all. A moral person must be able to say, "I can do this thing only if I could approve of everybody doing it."

That may be well and good. But aren't there exceptional circumstances or vocational differences that justify one person's doing something that would be met with disapproval if someone else were to do it? For example, it may be wrong to steal. But suppose you are lost in a wilderness blizzard and stumble upon an isolated cabin. Is it really wrong to break in and eat some of the available food? Perhaps not. But expressing this more deeply, in his *Critique of Practical Reason*, Kant explained the categorical imperative in this way: The only absolute good, the only thing that is good without qualification, is the goodwill. A person who wills the good, *is* good—even if he or she needs further help in deciding what the good is. On the other hand, even a really evil person can sometimes do good things, either unintentionally or out of some calculation of self-interest. In one of his poems, T. S. Eliot remarks in a Kantian spirit that "there is no greater treason than to do the right thing for the wrong reason," his point being that personal goodness is the centerpiece of ethics. Motivation is what counts; what we *want* is the important thing.

Well, we can agree with that, but it doesn't give us much to hold on to. We may be totally devoted to the good but have no clear idea about what the good is. So we return to the problem with which we started: People of goodwill have done despicable things, not by intention but by ignorance. Can Kant provide more help to us? He elaborated his principle by saying that we should always treat other persons as "ends" in themselves and not as "means" only. And, he asserted we cannot do this if we ever intentionally deceive another. This last point, put forth by Kant in his essay "The Supposed Right to Tell a Lie," has proved endlessly challenging to ethicists, who have offered various illustrations in which lying may represent a higher morality, such as hiding Jews during the Holocaust and lying about it to the authorities, as I noted earlier.

Leaving such debates aside, there is the larger question *why* Kant's categorical imperative—and the treatment of others as persons or ends, not means—is morally binding. Is there any ultimate grounding for this? There may be, at least in this: When we disobey the principle and treat other persons as "means" to our own ends—or as objects to be used by ourselves—we are in fact dehumanizing ourselves. To be authentically human ourselves, we must respect the humanity in others. When we dehumanize other people, we devalue the human in ourselves—a point demonstrated, interestingly, in Hegel's critique of slavery: By dehumanizing the slave, a slaveowner makes it impossible for the slave to affirm the slaveowner himself or herself as a fellow human being. Following this train of thought, the ultimate grounding of this form of ethics lies in our own essential humanity. The value we assign to other persons is but a reflection of the value we place upon ourselves.

This may appear to be a meaningful absolute upon which to ground ethics, grounded entirely in a version of natural law. But why does our personhood matter ultimately, except to ourselves? What are we to say to people who cannot value themselves in the first place? That they *ought* to? But why *ought* any of us value ourselves? "Brief and powerless is man's life," wrote Bertrand Russell, "on him and all his race the slow, sure doom falls pitiless and dark."[11] Yes indeed! Can our brief and powerless life, in itself, be the basis of ethics?

The quest for moral absolutes that move us beyond the sinkholes of pure relativism is certainly challenging, and I do not want to imply that these efforts are without merit. Indeed, though flawed, almost every point of view in ethics has *some* truth to it. But *absolute* truth? I think not. The problem, common to the views we have so quickly surveyed, is twofold. First, they do not convincingly relate us to an ultimate source of morality; second, they all have to be worked out in relation to the relativities we encounter in the real world. Facts can be maddeningly relative. But they are also inescapably important, for we live in a real world, not an abstract one.

GOD AS THE ABSOLUTE

What then is the ultimate source of morality? The Kantian perspective is quite suggestive, though also quite abstract. Universal law? What can that really be, and why does it matter? Good intention? Yes. Of course. But what is the "good" to which that refers, apart from the goodwill, which is also an abstraction? A Thomistic natural law of "ends"? All right, but by what moral logic can I rightly claim that one end is ultimately *better* than another, if the other suits my own purposes more? The end or purpose of the egg is to produce chickens, but maybe I prefer fried eggs. The end of sex is to produce children, but maybe I am more interested, most of the time, in the intimacy and companionship. Where, in all this, is there an *ultimate* that grounds human morality? So here's the difficulty with ethics: it requires detours and contains paradoxes. And we pause now over a central paradox in this debate over "relativism" vs. "absolutism": Is there a better way, one grounded more deeply in Christian ethics as a theological discipline?

I believe so. All of these questions point us back in a theological direction. As we have already observed, a truly rigorous ethics must include a value theory, and our immediate values have to be grounded in our center of value, what we value most. The ultimate center of value is what we worship. What we worship most is our god. Some gods are idols, but for a Christian the God revealed in Christ is our center of value.

The only conceivable absolute for Christian ethics is God, yet God transcends human comprehension. As Paul said, "Now we see in a mirror dimly." We're all bothered by the Taliban types, whether they are Muslims or Christians. They seem to know so much that they *cannot* know about God! Ultimately God is everything. But it is not given to us to *know* everything. Knowing the character of God is a formidable challenge to theologians; but isn't it really a challenge for all of us? How are we to identify what is absolutely true in our faith and ethics—and what is false or relative?

Our relationship with God, upon whom we are centered, is necessarily by faith, and we live in communities of faith that nurture and sustain and enlarge our faith. The Epistle to the Hebrews is surely right: "Now faith is the assurance of things hoped for, the conviction of things not seen" (11:1). Is that not a slender thread of absolute upon which to base our moral life? Maybe so. *But that is all anybody has!* As we live by faith in God, total certainty is elusive, but a kind of *certitude* becomes essential. We can be *convinced*, and live by our convictions, even while we recognize that God may yet lead us to some new thing, some new insight, some new possibilities. The saintly Mother Teresa may have provided us with the best illustration of this. Deeply devoted though she was to God and to her fellow human beings, her posthumously published memoir speaks frankly of her doubts. She was, in a sense, in a conversation with God—a God who might not even exist!—while devoting herself tirelessly to God's creatures in the unspeakable poverty of Calcutta. Is it possible to have a spiritual relationship with God even though we do not fully understand who God is or are not sure God exists?

Perhaps a simple human analogy will clarify things. We have friends, parents, children, brothers, sisters, spouses. Some we have known intimately for many years. Yet in even the most intimate of relationships, there is always something fresh and new to learn about the other person. So too with God. Through faith we have intimations about the God who is far above and beyond our knowledge. As Christians, we believe the reality of God is somehow disclosed in the person of Christ. For many Christians the heart of Christianity is the love of Christ, in which we find disclosed, through faith, the love of God. The essence of our faith is a kind of "hopeful love." We live in the hope that, at the center of all that is, there is one who relates to us in love.

How does this theological insight translate into living a moral life? One way to get at this is to speak of various doctrines such as grace, creation, or original sin as providing us with theological "entry points" into the moral life. They have a prima facie claim upon us, for they come to us as insight into our relationship with God. But these "entry points," gained from the long traditions of Christian life and thought, must encounter realities in the world. There we can test their applicability and limitations.

FACTS AND VALUES

It should be clear by now that moral decisions cannot be based upon facts alone. The British philosopher G. E. Moore described that approach as the "naturalistic fallacy," by which he meant the fallacy of believing that something is necessarily good just because it exists.[12] His argument may have been directed especially at the nineteenth-century British utilitarians (such as John Stuart Mill) who argued that the pleasure principle is the ultimate good, because it is what we most experience as being good. It's easy to agree that we experience pleasure (or happiness) as good and pain (or unhappiness) as evil. But what do the terms "good" or "evil" add to this psychological fact about our feelings? So we experience something as good. That means we like it. But it may be a long step from there to any kind of moral judgment. A psychological sadist may enjoy the sufferings of others, but does that make their suffering *good*? Most children would certainly enjoy a diet of excessive sweets. But is that good?

Moore's point is that even though something is a fact and undisputably real, this does not mean it is necessarily good. For example, a large majority may be revealed in a survey as greedy, but that does not mean that greed is good. Sometimes social ethics is mischaracterized as nothing more than "sociology," as though the secular science of sociology were a substitute for theologically grounded moral reasoning. Doubtless the social sciences have sometimes been taken to be a sufficient account of social ethics, but that misapprehension is another illustration of Moore's naturalistic fallacy. So what is *factually true* may be opposed to the good that ought to be. We may need to change what is! An authentic social ethics will be clear about that.

Before we can address the question of what needs to be changed—or what needs to be protected from the wrong kinds of changes—we need to know what is. A few examples may help explain what I mean: In the late 1930s the small town of Winchester, Ohio, debated whether or not to invest in a new town water supply. The town's drinking water came from wells, and there were enough of these to supply the needs of the community. Water for washing was typically collected from rooftops into cisterns—not good for drinking, but quite adequate for bathing and washing. It was the Depression, and the cost of the proposed water system, even with federal matching funds, would be a serious drain on local resources. Did they really need to do it? The primary reason the town was even investigating a new water system was an outbreak of typhoid fever from which some residents had died. Was there a connection, the town wondered, between the well water and the typhoid? That was a factual question. The moral issue seemed clear: Ending the threat of typhoid fever should have higher priority than other possible uses of community funds. Once the priority of the issue was established, the issue turned on determining the cause of the typhoid. Upon study, it became clear factually that contaminated drinking water had caused the disease, and so the town eventually invested in the new water system. For the town not to make this investment would have been morally wrong.

Yet another illustration: At a panel discussion at the University of Delaware in the 1980s, the well-known environmentalist Garrett Hardin advanced his theory of what he called "lifeboat ethics" to govern national policy in providing foreign aid to needy countries.[13] According to his analogy, people of the more prosperous countries—like the United States—are in a lifeboat in a stormy sea. There is room in the lifeboat for some of the other people who are struggling in the waves, but that room is limited. If we try to save everybody, we will only capsize the boat, and all will be lost. It makes sense, he argued, to concentrate on helping only those societies with a prospect of "making it." The speaker then stated, as a factual conclusion, that India cannot "make it" and sending foreign aid to India will do no good there and can only weaken us here. This was a pretty extraordinary factual claim, that India couldn't make it. The speaker was, of course, quite in error. Today India has one of the fastest-growing economies in the world. Moreover, he had offered (even for that time, before India began to take off economically) an extraordinary oversimplification of the economic possibilities of a nation of nearly a billion people. But his view did dramatize the value of careful economic research, both into the possibilities of economic growth in third-world countries and into the economic realities of the wealthier nations of Europe and North America.

The big debate in the United States in 2003 over the wisdom of military intervention in Iraq centered originally over the factual question whether the dictatorial government of Saddam Hussein had weapons of mass destruction (and a program to develop nuclear bombs) with an intent to use them to threaten Western countries. The war began on the factual premise that this was the case. When it became clear that supposed facts initially presented to support the U.S. action were unfounded, equally erroneous "facts" were offered to justify the invasion. The alleged facts would not have affected the judgment of most pacifist Christians—they would have opposed military action in any case. But for others, doubtless including a vast majority of the people of the United States and Europe, facts were of paramount importance.

Factual determinations are also important in deciding whether proposed changes would do more harm than good. The medical adage "First, do no harm" makes the point. Surgery is itself life-threatening; sometimes medications will do more harm than good. These are factual issues. From Thomas Aquinas we get the moral principle that even a perfectly moral policy, adopted out of the best intentions, should not be undertaken if it is altogether unenforceable. Let's use the great American prohibition experiment as an illustration. The prohibition of the sale of alcoholic beverages climaxed a long campaign by temperance groups—mostly related to Protestant churches—to combat the visible evils of drunkenness upon health and family life. Whether or not the goal was based upon defensible moral reasoning, the policy proved to be utterly unenforceable, and its actual result was an increase in lawlessness and overall disrespect for the law itself. Again, the likely effects of a policy, while not always completely predictable, are quite relevant to the moral question of what should be done.

In getting facts, it is an interesting question whether ethics should take account of the behavioral sciences, with their limited but very real capacity to predict group behavior. Politicians do not have the luxury of ignoring predictable group behavior, and sometimes their intuitive grasp of social attitudes is more accurate than academic studies. The fact that social attitudes may not be at all amenable to proposed changes or that the public may support changes that, for purely ethical reasons, are not desirable, can pose powerful dilemmas for leaders seeking to provide morally enlightened leadership. Such dilemmas raise difficult decisions about when to compromise and when not to, and how to resist making concessions that would support a situation that seems obviously wrong.

Two Arkansas leaders found themselves in such dilemmas, and their contrasting stories will serve as illustration. One, Senator J. William Fulbright, was confronted in the late 1950s with the dilemma of whether to support or oppose the racist attitudes of both a majority of American citizens and his Southern colleagues in the U.S. Senate. Fulbright had made important contributions to international understanding, such as his authorship of the Fulbright Scholar program. He knew that his continued presence in the Senate was necessary for the sake of a more enlightened U.S. foreign policy. If he were to vote in favor of desegregation, he believed he would undoubtedly lose the next election, and his important perspective on foreign affairs would be lost. So, without much enthusiasm, he chose to support racial segregation.

The other public figure was Congressman Brooks Hays. Confronted with the same dilemma during the crisis over racial desegregation of the Little Rock, Arkansas, high school in 1958, he refused to support the continuation of segregation—and promptly lost his seat in Congress. I believe he made the more discerning moral decision, although I have enormous respect for all that Senator Fulbright was able to accomplish related to U.S. foreign policy (including his resolute questioning of the Vietnam War). But while facts do not in themselves make values, they are inescapably relevant to moral decision-making.

INDIVIDUAL INTEGRITY
AND COMMUNAL AUTHORITY

Yes, moral decisions have to be made. But who should make them? Our discussion thus far implies that all of us, as individuals, have that responsibility—although community policy decisions obviously are made, in some fashion, by the community. Do we deliberate about the issues personally and then decide, either for ourselves or as we participate in the community decision-making?

Or do we, in some fashion, rely upon the authority of the community in arriving at our own views?

Most of us are strongly influenced by the views of the groups and communities with which we self-identify. Psychologically, it is very difficult to dissent from group moral consensus when the group is made up of people whose approval we value, particularly if that consensus appears to be unanimous. At the same time it is very easy to conform to group pressure. Even courageous dissenters often cave in after a while. That may be the most important reason why moral values acquired early in life tend to stick, family nurture being what it is, and why conversions from one religion to another are relatively uncommon.

But are we nothing more than units in a social whole, a collective that arrives at judgments that then determine our personal views? A group, while it acts as a whole, is still made up of individuals, and the formation of group consensus is often preceded by interactions among its members. The opinions of leaders may carry greater weight, but in most settings leaders have to take the views of members into account. Groups do change, through time, and it is often the lonely dissenter who leads the way, although being in dissent can be painful.

This relationship between individual and group is an enduring polarity. We are all both individual and social by nature. One hundred percent individualism is quite impossible; but a society cannot exist without *some* independence among its individual members. The relationship of independence to collective conformity doubtless varies with individuals, time, and situations.

The bearing of these observations on moral decision-making is profound. If the heart of our moral values is religious in character, then we truly are dependent in large measure upon the communities of faith and tradition of which we are a part—even among those who are in rebellion against their communities of origin. How are a community's values expressed? Largely through its traditions, passed on from generation to generation, with some deviations and modifications through time. From this perspective, sacred Scriptures are a part—doubtless the most important part—of these traditions. The authority of the Bible, for instance, is ultimately derived from the community that accepted its writings as normative and has been formed by it. In that sense, biblical authority is derived from church authority, and church authority is conferred and confirmed by the Christian community as it has existed through the centuries. Such a view of authority may not conform to more fundamentalist conceptions of the Bible, but is it not self-evidently true? The fundamentalist perspective, discussed earlier, hardly considers the relationship between the emerging early Christian community and the canonization of its Scriptures. Such a perspective may ultimately rest upon the simple assertion that biblical writers and the early church were inspired by the Holy Spirit. But that perspective certainly leaves plenty of room for the relativities of inspiration.

So communal authority, as expressed by Bible and tradition as well as contemporary moral judgments, remains basic. Such authority is more dynamic than biblical fundamentalism, arguably serving the true authority of God more faithfully.

THE TRANSCENDENT ABSOLUTE

If God alone is the true absolute, then we can never gain absolute closure on the moral questions we face—except, perhaps, when our moral judgments are expressed in abstract form, such as that we should be people of goodwill. But that does not mean we are left without moral convictions. Some of those convictions are drawn from the past, for we are inheritors of great, illuminating traditions pointing us toward what is true and good. While any time-bound formulation of the meaning of those traditions may be subject to error, we live in the confidence that on the whole they do point to what is true and good. Thus, as Christians we live by our commitment to love, as manifested in the life and teachings of Jesus Christ—even while we remain open to new insight into what love means. Put differently, we live in the expectation that God may have a new word to offer all of us in each succeeding generation. That word can speak to each of us as individuals, but it is deepened and enriched as we converse with one another in community.

So we are not left without an absolute foundation as we address the hard questions. But the absolute is not in the conclusions we reach or in the traditions to which we respond. The absolute is the transcendent God whose will we struggle to understand and express through our decisions and actions. We have abundant resources in our efforts to understand the purposes of God. But none of these resources is, in itself, to be taken as absolute.

Many people will turn immediately to the rich fabric of ethical rules as the primary resource. So we must give special consideration to the place of rules in arriving at our moral decisions.

RULES AND RELATIONSHIPS

I have postponed until now a question that might occur to many readers: Isn't ethics basically about rules to guide our conduct? There are different opinions about this among Christians, including professional Christian ethicists. The usefulness of ethical rules is not necessarily in conflict with our faith in God as the transcendent basis of the moral life. But there is an important difference between framing ethics around rules and seeing the heart of ethics to be about relationships—to God and to the rest of humanity and God's creation. If our relationship with God is determined by our obedience to rules that God has set forth—however these rules are to be known—then the heart of ethics is knowing and obeying those rules. The will of God, set forth in rules, is to be our guide. That is the view of very many Christians; indeed, most Christians probably employ the language of rules when discussing the moral life. On the other hand, if our relationship with God lies in responding to God's love, as that love is expressed theologically by the grace we have received through Jesus Christ, then morality is about a life of love. Moral rules, which draw together the wisdom of the ages about how best to live the life of love, can be very helpful. But there can be a huge difference between treating love as only helping us better to obey the rules and regarding rules as being in the service of love—helping us to serve and fulfill loving relationships.

In the twentieth century, Christian ethicists spent much effort trying to clarify and illuminate such distinctions. Joseph Fletcher, in his widely read *Situation Ethics*,[14] directly subordinated rules to love. We are, in his view, to do what love requires in the situation, then and there. The only "law" is the law of love, which is more love than law. Fletcher's strong emphasis on love was for many readers a welcome relief from rigid rules and moralism and clearly expressed the central ethical theme of the New Testament. But his critics, such as Paul Ramsey,[15] were quick to point out that Fletcher did not provide any criteria to help us understand what *is* the most loving thing to do, a criticism also levied against Paul Lehmann's influential 1963 volume, *Ethics in a Christian Context*. Both Fletcher and Lehmann relied heavily upon intuition, and seemed to presume that if we are truly loving and clearly Christian, we will just *know* what to do! Such an approach may be better at the motivational side of ethics than it is in discernment of what needs to be done to fulfill that motivation.

Various Christian ethical traditions have relied much more heavily upon rules, laws, and principles. The Boston personalist moral-law tradition, first developed by the philosopher Edgar S. Brightman and then elaborated upon by ethicist Walter G. Muelder and theologian L. Harold DeWolf, constructed an elaborate scheme of moral laws, grounded in the basic value of the human person and intended to guide the conduct of people of goodwill, not just Christians. The laws attempted to combine flexibility with principles such as the need to be relevant to specific situations and always to do the "best possible." I have found this set of moral principles to be especially useful in discussions of business ethics and political ethics, where it is often possible to consider issues more abstractly. But the very abstractness of the principles is part of the problem. How do we

continue to place love at the center? That is, how do we give sufficient regard to motivation? Is there a tendency in such a table
of moral laws to make obedience to the laws itself the norm?

Ethicist Paul Ramsey, offering yet another solution to the conflict between rules and love, observed that some rules in themselves, objectively, embody love. Ramsey contrasted this idea,
which he called "rule agapism" (derived from the Greek New Testament word *agapē*, self-giving love), with "act agapism." Act
agapism, or acts directly motivated by Christian love, means acting out of personal, individual motivation to do good for others
in any given situation.[16] "Rules of practice," Ramsey's precise
phrase, meant a set of rules that determine a general sphere of
human activity. Marriage, for instance, entails a body of "rules of
practice" that in themselves embody love. Personal commitment
and emotional attachment as expressions of love are quite important, of course, but the institution itself supports and sustains
those expressions.

Similarly, Ramsey believed, we could speak of laws as
embodying justice. Even when people are not motivated by any
concern for justice, the laws can be said to embody love.
Pre–civil-rights-era laws in southern states that mandated segregation could be said to have embodied the opposite of love. By
being a normal, law-abiding citizen in such states, one was objectively doing unloving things—even if one personally harbored no
racial ill will. On the other hand, laws requiring businesses to
serve all and guaranteeing equal access to voting, embodied the
community's regard and *were* an objective form of love, even as
they governed the behavior of people who were thoroughly racist.

So, sustaining different kinds of rules of practice that objectively embody love is a loving thing to do. But how do we
know which rules have this effect? Following the suggestion of
William Frankena, Ramsey refers to "summary rule agapism,"
which, put most simply, means that rules can be known to
embody love if they summarize the past experience of people
attempting to express love in particular kinds of situations. In
fact, many rules are of this sort, and just as individuals learn
from experience what seems to work best in expressing love, so

a whole community of faith can develop rules that express its corporate experience through time.

There is, however, another point that must be considered as we relate rules to relationships: When one's ethic is primarily focused on obedience to rules for their own sake, the motivation is externalized, and good moral behavior becomes our obedience to commands from others. Why should we do something? Because our parents told us to. Because the church told us to. Because we are told by others that God told us to. Our motive may not be to do good for its own sake, but rather to do what is right so we will be rewarded and not punished. Ironically, our moral focus has become selfish: We have obeyed the rule in order to serve ourselves. Paul's anguished admission of his inability to fulfill the law points toward this. We can obey the law perfectly but still fall far short of love.

But not all obedience to moral law is self-centered. Classical theological reflection has identified three uses of the law. The first is to guard us from unthinkingly injuring ourselves and others. The second is to experience despair at our inability to obey, and thus be forced in our weakness to turn to God's grace with trust. The third use of the law, and the one relevant to our discussion, is to guide our conduct as we seek sincerely to respond lovingly to the love of God. When the law becomes habitual in our lives, it can lead us to do good *instinctively*. Ideally we have become mature to the point of no longer being capable of some kinds of conduct that are hurtful, while doing good things without giving it a second thought.

Despite the importance, historically and actually, of moral laws, loving relationship remains at the center of our ethics—love from and to God and in human relationships. But now we must address the central problem of this book: Even with the immense background of moral wisdom embodied in the traditions of our faith communities, and even with the best of goodwill, we can still be puzzled in the face of our responsibilities in the real world. How are we to translate this theologically inspired love into the good that we intend? In the next chapter, I will turn directly to this, the central problem of this book.

4

The Moral Burden of Proof

How then can we think about the moral decisions we face? Our basic values, grounded in religious faith, and the influences of the groups of which we are a part remain basic and formative. But moral decision-making cannot be exclusively intuitive. Are there ways of thinking that proved helpful in the past and can promise better moral discernment in the future? Can we find a way to be decisive while remaining open-minded? Can we have moral convictions without closing our minds to new insight? Is there a way we can address dilemmas and uncertainties that, at the end of the day, remain unclear—even though we still must act? Can we find approaches to moral decision-making that, while not ensuring agreement, at least provide greater clarity about our disagreements and increase the likelihood of consensus later on in the face of new evidence and greater insight?

A LEGAL ANALOGY

I doubt whether any method of moral judgment can achieve perfection at all of these points. But the methods employed in courts of law have shown themselves to be fruitful and can serve as a model. When cases come before a court they are, in principle, not yet decided. Characteristically two opposing sides confront the judge and jury with their differing versions of the facts and how those facts should be interpreted. Evidence is presented, arguments are heard. In the end, a decision must be made, even if the conflict has not been clearly resolved.

One approach, typical in civil conflict, is for the court to rely upon the preponderance of the evidence: if, for example, 55 percent of the evidence seems to support one side while only 45 percent supports the other, then the first side wins—even though some doubt may remain. Behind this lies a complex set of rules governing what kinds of evidence count in different kinds of situations. There are times, however, when a decision turns on which witnesses the court finds most credible, along with other kinds of factual evidence. Ideally the court will follow objective rules and procedures faithfully and weigh the evidence carefully enough so that the outcome will transcend purely subjective ways of deciding.

A more helpful approach, used typically in criminal cases and often in civil cases, is to clarify the legal presumption. The term "presumption" means what we assume to be true until there is sufficient evidence to set our presumption aside. Thus, in American jurisprudence, a person charged with a criminal offense is *presumed* to be not guilty until his or her guilt has been proved beyond reasonable doubt. The decision centers upon whether the prosecution has met that standard with its evidence. Has it demonstrated sufficiently that the presumption of innocence must give way to the opposite conclusion? Notice two things about this process. First, it provides a basis for arriving at a conclusion even when the evidence is not conclusive. This is not a "preponderance of the evidence" approach, and to put it mathematically, a 75 percent likelihood of guilt is not enough. "Beyond reasonable doubt" may not equal 100 percent, so that there is still some room for subjective judgment, but the burden of proof still rests with the prosecution.

The second point is that the defense does not even have to mount a case by producing evidence or calling witnesses if the prosecution has not established guilt conclusively—if it has not met this burden of proof. The defense does not have to prove *anything*, unless, of course, the prosecution case is so strong that it must be contested in detail. Ideally a prosecutor will not seek to indict an accused person unless the case is strong enough to make a conviction likely. But the prosecutor's judgment about a person's guilt is far from the final judgment. That will rest with the jury.

The importance of presumption and burden of proof was illustrated in a case in central California during the 1960s. A local businessman was shot. With him at the time was a business associate who claimed that the man had committed suicide. The gunshot wound was inflicted by a rifle, not a pistol, however, which made the suicide claim doubtful. After thorough investigation and due consideration, no indictment was sought. When the county attorney was asked whether he thought the death was suicide or murder, he admitted he still wasn't sure, but there was not enough clear evidence to gain a conviction against the associate. The defense wouldn't have had to prove his innocence; rather, it would have been the government's burden to prove his guilt. Despite the doubt, a decision had to be made, and, in accordance with law, the potential defendant got the benefit of the doubt.

This is—or should always be—the case with criminal proceedings. While civil cases are often resolved by a preponderance of the evidence, a presumed outcome is involved in some instances even here. A personal illustration: Years ago, one of my sons did some work on a Maryland farm, and his payment was an old Spanish motorcycle. The motorcycle had no title, registration, or even serial number. I accompanied my son to the motor vehicles department of our city, Washington, D.C., to see about title and registration—fully expecting a very long, involved process. To our surprise, the title and registration were quickly arranged. Why? In the absence of any counter-claim of ownership, my son's possession of the vehicle was sufficient. Possession carried the legal presumption of ownership.

APPLYING THE IDEA OF "PRESUMPTION" TO ETHICAL DECISION-MAKING

There are, of course, significant differences between legal and moral decisions. But the legal method of presumption and evidence can be applied to the hard choices we confront in ethical decision-making. As I have defined this elsewhere, a moral presumption is a norm or value or belief on the basis of which one will act unless sufficient evidence can be shown that one should not.[17] Sometimes in ethical decision-making, as in legal proceedings, we can be guided by a "preponderance of the evidence." That is often the case when choosing between different ways of achieving a specific goal. For instance, a patient and physician have decided that seeking a cure for a particular kind of cancer is morally compelling. That is a given. But whether to use surgery or chemotherapy or radiation treatments will likely depend upon a factual assessment of which is most likely to be effective. There may be no need to inject a bias or presumption into the decision.

But many, if not most, of the quandaries we confront can be clarified by deciding where to place the presumption or burden of proof. The burden of proof must be borne by actions that are contrary to the norms or values that we assume to be most in accord with our beliefs.

The best illustration of this approach in Christian ethics may be in the uses of just-war theory. The just-war tradition does not (contrary to popular misconception) glorify war. Quite the contrary, it considers war to be evil, to be engaged in only as a very last resort when it is clear that the alternatives would be even worse. The burden of proof, for Christians, falls on those who are *for* war. The just-war tradition, dating at least from Saint Augustine in the fifth century, elaborated the conditions that might meet the test in favor of war: Is it in response to an act of aggression? Is it a last resort after all peaceable means have been attempted? Is there a reasonable prospect of victory? If a military action does not meet all of the tests, it is to be avoided.

While the just-war tradition may be the best illustration of how this use of presumption in moral decision-making has been developed and applied in Christian history, there are other areas where it could be applicable, divorce, for example. Marriage was long considered an absolute value, and divorce was to be avoided at all cost (although in Matt. 5:32 Jesus is represented as allowing for an exception in cases of adultery). In recent years most Protestant churches have departed from the absolute prohibition of divorce, and even the Roman Catholic Church, while holding to a more absolute position, allows for the annulment of a marriage if it can be shown never to have been a real marriage—a very wide loophole. At least implicitly churches continue to regard divorce as a last resort, since their wedding ceremonies continue to incorporate the lifelong commitment "until death does us part." So far, at least, there has been no generally accepted list of criteria or conditions justifying exceptions to the presumption in favor of continuing a marriage. Such a list, if developed, would doubtless include things like spousal abuse and abandonment.

Other illustrations can be offered. For instance, from 1988 to 1992 the United Methodist Church conducted a study process on the highly inflamed issue of homosexuality. In 1972 the denomination had adopted a clearly stated social principle that "we do not condone the practice of homosexuality and consider this practice incompatible with Christian teaching." For the next sixteen years, efforts to change this language failed at each of the subsequent General Conferences of the church. The committee charged with studying this matter held hearings, consulted experts, and pursued other studies. As it concluded its work, there remained substantial disagreement among the committee's twenty-four members. All were agreed that the next General Conference should modify the statement in the denomination's Social Principles by acknowledging that the church had not been able to arrive at a common mind on the compatibility of homosexual practice with Christian faith. But there was a clear division on the committee between those who held that the present state of knowledge "does not provide a satisfactory basis upon which the church can responsibly maintain the condemnation of all homosexual practice" and those who took the view that the state of knowledge "does not provide a satisfactory basis upon which the church can responsibly alter its previously held position."[18] The presumption for the first group was against the traditional condemnation, while the presumption for the others was against change. Here was clear evidence, within a church body, of contrasting presumptions. But it was also an illustration of the way in which clearly stating differences of presumptions can clarify differences of opinion.

Another illustration of moral presumption is professional confidentality, a nearly absolute principle among therapists, lawyers, and clergy. State laws recognize the principle completely for lawyers and except in unusual circumstances for clergy, so that usually neither can be compelled to reveal confidences as witnesses in court. Usually. But, at least in the case of clergy, in many states knowledge of child abuse gained confidentially must be reported to authorities. So the presumption is strongly in favor of the maintaining of confidences, but some exceptions are identified.

In more general terms, truth telling is a very important moral presumption, although there is disagreement about whether it is absolute. As I noted earlier, the philosopher Immanuel Kant considered it to be an absolute, with no exceptions. But other ethicists, while respecting truth telling as a compelling moral presumption, do not regard it as an absolute and raise serious questions. Would telling the truth in a given situation place somebody's life in jeopardy? Would it unnecessarily disrupt a relationship? Would it lead to other consequences more damaging than the damage caused by losses of credibility when untruthfulness became known? Even among those who are not prepared to make an absolute out of truth telling, there must still be high respect for it as a norm, for as Kant had observed, the loss of confidence in truthfulness severely undermines normal human relationships and diminishes the fabric of trust within the human community. Winston Churchill is supposed to have said that truth is such a precious thing that it must be protected by a battalion of lies. Though typical of his witticisms, such a remark evidenced his (and many other political leaders') primary focus upon actual results. In the exceptional circumstances of World War II, one might have reflected in this vein about deceptions needed for military purposes—to mislead the enemy about one's intentions, for instance. Perhaps that is yet another reason why war itself is so questionable from a moral standpoint.

MORAL PRESUMPTIONS AS A COMMON STARTING POINT

Although there is nothing startlingly new about the use of presumptions as a starting point in moral decision-making, the fact that our presumptions are so rarely examined may mean that we have not given serious thought to the hard choices we face. Consider a couple of general illustrations of how we often use moral presumptions in our decision-making, particularly in our reliance upon external moral authority or expert opinion.

Perhaps the most obvious example is the way we are guided by dominant authorities. We may believe we are altogether independent in our decision-making; in fact, we rely heavily upon the judgments of others—for example, if we are deeply committed members of a community of faith, such as a church. We may not be entirely convinced that its leaders should be followed on all moral questions, but if we respect their leadership and share the same values, we will take their judgment quite seriously. At a local level, this is why sermons on moral questions can have considerable influence upon worshiping parishioners. I find it very revealing that those who disagree with a stance taken from the pulpit are often deeply upset. If sermon pronouncements simply did not matter, why would anybody get exercised about them? In effect, the minister or priest or rabbi or imam is saying that this is what the faith we share means, when applied to this or that problem. People may feel free to disagree, but many will give the benefit of the doubt to what has been said, especially if it has been articulated cogently and related clearly to the shared faith tradition. A statement offered by a denominational authority—such as a council of bishops, or a Roman Catholic pope, or a denominational assembly—may claim similar status, although with uneven degrees of acceptance. There may be other friends and relatives whose views are taken with similar seriousness. We presume they're right unless we are convinced by enough evidence that they're not.

Our ordinary uses of presumption are shown in how we deal with experts in solving ordinary, practical problems. We're likely to consider seriously the authority of a properly certified professional—such as a plumber, electrician, auto mechanic, or physician. Few people accept the authority of such professionals without question, but their judgment is the starting point, the presumption. Often such experts are considered authoritative in their judgments on moral issues related to their fields of expertise. For instance, an economist may be granted a certain presumption or moral authority in dealing with questions related to poverty or world trade. But persons who are expert on factual questions may not share our basic moral values. The factual side has to be related to the value side. An economist, for example, who obviously has no concern about poverty will not have as much influence with people whose religious faith leads them to care about the plight of the poor. It is easier to take seriously an expert's recommendation about the means to be employed if one is also confident that that expert shares the same ends. But the point remains that most of us really do delegate much of our decision-making to those whose judgment we respect and whom we consider to be better equipped than we are to suggest how to implement our values. The authorities we presume to be right can matter very much.

Similarly, the ideological perspectives that shape our minds matter. An ideology is a governing set of values combined with views of how things actually work. For instance, in this country and in much of the rest of the world, the idea of political democracy has just this sort of influence on the way we think, even though we may not have a carefully thought-out understanding of what the term means. In general the idea of "democracy" may just come down to belief that a majority should rule and that there should be full freedom of expression for those seeking to support or oppose public policies. A more refined understanding of democracy will include belief in a wide range of human rights that support equality within the community. But in any case, those who believe in democracy will, consciously or unconsciously, give it this presumptive status.

Some situations may not be ready for a full flowering of democracy, but the burden of proof must be borne by those who oppose it or deviate from it. In recent years much has been made of the efforts by the Bush administration to push for democracy in the Arab world. Success in this has, at best, been so limited that many have concluded that it is a mistake, that the push has been too soon and too hard. In effect, for skeptics, the burden of proof has been met to set aside the normal presumption.

Closer to home, however, judgments about fairness in elections are almost entirely at the level of what will best guarantee fairness and not about whether full democracy is the moral goal. For years, for example, the citizens of the District of Columbia have chafed under their lack of regular voting representation in Congress. Full democracy would clearly require representation in Congress like that of citizens of the fifty states, since District of Columbia citizens are fully citizens of the United States. Several efforts to gain representation have been mounted over the past three decades. Opponents do not question the ideology of democracy. But, implicitly treating this as a presumption and not an absolute, they argue that the burden of proof in opposing full democratic rights for D.C. citizens is met by the constitutional provision that representation is by states. Implicitly, the Constitution is accorded a higher level of presumption than democracy. (The democratic good faith of such opposition may, of course, be called into question by the fact that such opponents have not visibly advocated a constitutional amendment or some other way of satisfying the objections.)

Other ideological presumptions include the economic ideologies of laissez-faire capitalism and the various forms of socialism.

The late economist Milton Friedman, a deeply committed capitalist, long supported open-market, free-enterprise solutions to economic issues. That was his clear presumption. He was, however, willing to acknowledge that some necessary exceptions can bear the burden of proof; so he advocated the negative income tax as a way of supplying direct welfare grants to qualifying poor people. Socialists, in contrast, presume the superiority of state control of the economy, but may support exceptions to that where the free-market principle appears best suited to solve particular economic problems. I find it fascinating, for instance, that in China, long committed to a Maoist version of Marxian communism, the market principle has been allowed to flourish, with numbers of Chinese entrepreneurs becoming quite wealthy in the process. The Communist Party retains political control, including overall control of the economy, but deviations from the socialist ideology are everywhere to be seen.

Other forms of ideology may occur to you. Sometimes ideological differences follow party lines. Broadly speaking, in the United States the Democratic Party is more supportive of governmental interventions to assure greater equality, while the Republican Party is more committed to free enterprise. But political leaders of both parties are more than willing to deviate from these ideological generalities when necessary to solve obvious problems and to secure votes from less ideologically influenced voters. So it is safe to say that presumptions are at work, along with a provision for deviating from them when it appears necessary.

I have, in this chapter, avoided use of a term that, properly understood, means the same thing as "presumption." The word is "prejudice." Derived from Latin, "prejudice" means prejudgment. It is the judgment we make before considering the evidence. I have avoided the term here because of its association with racial prejudice, although racial prejudice often illustrates exactly the point I am trying to make. Such prejudice is a prejudgment that persons of a chosen, stigmatized race are evil or at least inferior to persons of one's own race. For some highly racist people, the judgment is so absolute that it admits no exceptions. But for others, it may mean that while people of the supposedly inferior race are on the whole to be treated as inferiors, there may be some exceptions who can bear the burden of proving their acceptability. So you may hear, "So-and-so is a good representative of his/her 'race,' perhaps because he/she knows his/her 'place.'" Or so-and-so is a "credit to his/her race." Such language was quite common in the racist and anti-Semitic culture of America a generation or so ago, and it is not unknown today, although people may be quieter about it.

Since presumptions (or prejudices) can be based upon wrong-headed values—as is so often the case—we must be all the more careful about the values we carry into such decision-making. Christians, along with other persons of goodwill, need to examine their inherited and culturally informed presumptions rigorously. I believe it is possible to frame our presumptions on the basis of the deepest values of our religious traditions. There is much room for disagreement among Christians, to say nothing of the divergent opinions among persons of other faith traditions and those who are purely secular in outlook. Still, as we struggle with the question of which moral values should have this central place in our decision-making, we bring greater clarity to our own moral choices and to our conversation with those whose views are different. To this task we now turn.

5

Basic Moral Presumptions

I can, easily enough, state the *basic* moral presumption with which I believe most Christians would be in agreement: In all of our decisions we should place the burden of proof against anything that is contrary to Christian faith. But that is too broad to be helpful. The very fact that Christians so often disagree about basic values might tell us that there is need for greater precision in identifying Christian moral presumptions. Is it possible to give different aspects or elements of the faith the weight of presumption, so that we can at least know what we are agreeing or disagreeing about? In what follows, I will offer a number of possibilities, knowing that any such identification of presumptions must be incomplete and that some Christians disagree with some of these as I will state them.

USES OF SCRIPTURE

Many Christians would begin the quest for moral presumptions by turning to Scripture. Laying aside the difficult issue of the authority of Scripture, they might say that every commandment or rule expressed in the Bible should at least get the benefit of the doubt. The Ten Commandments say that we should not kill. Perhaps there are circumstances justifying killing, but those circumstances should at least have to bear the burden of proof. Similarly we should not steal, bear false witness, or commit adultery, and setting these commandments aside should also bear the burden of proof. But while such commandments are easily framed to carry great weight as presumptions, there are other biblical commandments that we can reject out of hand. For instance, in Deuteronomy we are told that "those born of an illicit union shall not be admitted to the assembly of the LORD. Even to the tenth generation, none of their descendants shall be admitted to the assembly of the LORD" (Deut. 23:2). And Leviticus specifies that "one who blasphemes the name of the LORD shall be put to death; the whole congregation shall stone the blasphemer" (Lev. 24:16). Apparently by divine command, the Israelite judge Samuel ordered King Saul to kill all the Amalekites—men, women, and children, plus all of their animals. Saul's failure to do so led to his rejection by the Lord. That, and Joshua's destruction of Jericho, are biblical accounts of divinely ordered genocide. And in the NT Paul assigned inferior status to women and, on a more trivial note, required that men should not wear their hair long. I believe such moral prescriptions are flatly contradictory to the deeper insights of the Bible; they even help to account for the rejection of Christian tradition by morally sensitive twenty-first-century people.

There are, of course, many biblical rules and requirements that can be taken much more seriously than these. But how are we to distinguish between biblical rules and precedents that should be given presumptive weight and those that ought not to be given any status at all?

The most satisfactory answer is that we cannot take biblical rules simply at face value just because they are in the Bible. Rather, we should respond to the deep biblical message from which the heart of our faith is derived. The ideas of God's transcendence and God's goodness as revealed in Christ are the best starting points: God is greater than we are, and God is love.

Another way to put this is that our starting point should be biblical theology, as refined and elaborated through Christian history, rather than particular rules taken at face value.

The ethical task of every generation of Christians is to struggle with the moral presumptions drawn from the faith tradition that are most relevant to the problems actually faced. In addressing this task, we discover that the legacy of Christian tradition is richly applicable to situations today. Many of our inherited doctrines can be expressed as moral presumptions, and we can follow their guidance as directly and creatively as possible, deviating only when the presumption in favor of such doctrines must be set aside for the sake of the deeper implications of the faith. By the same token, when presumptions appear to be in conflict with one another, we are pushed to see them in the perspective of the deepest insights of our faith.

By way of illustration, I wish now to suggest a number of presumptions that can be drawn more or less directly from a Christian faith perspective. Some of these represent basic, positive values; others represent theological insights into the limitations presented by human nature and what Christians call original sin. Still others note complementary values that must be kept in balance.

POSITIVE CHRISTIAN VALUE PRESUMPTIONS

Most of the doctrinal affirmations of Christian faith can, in one way or another, be translated into that language of moral presumptions: faith-based assumptions that are given the benefit of the doubt when challenged in moral decision-making. I will single out six of these as being particularly relevant to us as we face the hard questions in the twenty-first century.

1. A presumption for grace. Absolutely essential to the theology of most Christians is the grace of God, as expressed through Jesus Christ. The word "grace," employed by the apostle Paul, is drawn from Roman jurisprudence: grace was a pardon granted an accused person whose guilt had been established, so that grace meant not being punished when one deserved to be. In Paul's theological appropriation of the term, grace means God's full acceptance of sinners, despite their deserving punishment. It is giving people what they do not deserve. It is being forgiven. Moreover, the implication, drawn clearly in Christian Scripture, is that we should pass this grace along, as the Lord's Prayer advises, "Forgive us our sins as we forgive those who have sinned against us." To put it more boldly, while God's grace is freely given to undeserving people, it is not possible for one to receive that grace, that love, from God, unlovingly.

Translated into a moral presumption, that means we act with grace toward others as directly as we can, setting aside the fact that other people may not deserve this gift. When in doubt, this means that in our interpersonal relationships we are to forgive and be patient with the imperfections of other people. I don't pretend for a moment that that is always easy or that I myself am very good at it! But forgiveness is fundamental to the faith of Christians. Jesus' admonition to love one's enemies can be taken to mean that our *attitude* should be informed by grace, without exception. Most compellingly, Jesus uttered words of forgiveness for his executioners, even while suffering terrible agony on the cross. If such an incontestably good man as Jesus could express such grace, is that not all the more reason why the rest of us should work at being more forgiving?

If this is the case, then why should we speak of grace in personal relationships as a presumption and not an absolute moral imperative? So far as our own attitude is concerned, perhaps grace truly is nearly an absolute. But saying that is the same as saying that we should be persons of absolute goodwill and be guided absolutely by love. The problem is that sometimes our attitude of grace may lead us to take actions that do not seem to be a direct expression of love. These situations should be the exception, not the rule, in our decision-making. The exceptions come in the way that that grace is expressed. For instance, while our presumption should be to express grace and not judgment, those who have injured others should not be led to believe that the injury has not mattered. A healthy marriage, for example, must be saturated with grace on both sides; neither husband nor wife should be slow to apologize or to forgive. But not all marriages are healthy. Persistent disrespectful behavior should not be rewarded with simple acceptance—for in the process the slighted partner stores up resentments, the disrespectful partner cannot grow morally, and the marriage becomes more and more unhealthy. This is even truer in the case of spousal abuse, which should never be tolerated. It is not an expression of love for the abused to tolerate the abuse; a better way to show grace is to insist upon effective counseling and, in some cases, to separate or divorce. In such situations, and in others where toleration of misconduct is enabling a person to continue in a destructive—and self-destructive—pattern, one does not want to engage in what Dietrich Bonhoeffer called "cheap grace." To Bonhoeffer, "cheap grace" is a sentimental form of love that ignores real problems and avoids personal sacrifice. That isn't really grace at all.

Still, the presumption remains for expressing grace in the most direct possible ways. This expression can even take a negative, but creative form, such as a group of friends and loved ones confronting an alcoholic or drug addict with what his addiction is doing to destroy himself and his relationships. Such confrontations often provide creative avenues and resources for healing. They are a kind of tough love. But the accent still must be more on "love" than on "tough."

Grace, as a theologically grounded presumption, is also applicable to some collective decisions. Can a whole community exercise grace? Probably not, if we mean a simultaneous and unanimous outpouring of grace. But bearing in mind that few if any policies of any society are supported unanimously, the policies of a whole community can *express* grace. The famous Truth and Reconciliation Commission of South Africa, for example, certainly represented a society's policy of grace. After the collapse of racial apartheid and the election of President Nelson Mandela, the question was what should be done to punish the many inhumanities of the previous apartheid regime. Many wanted to identify perpetrators and mete out harsh penalties, but President Mandela and Archbishop Desmond Tutu chose instead to exercise grace: Those who had been responsible for the atrocities would be given amnesty if they would come before the Commission and freely and accurately confess what they had done. The confession was the "tough" part; the amnesty was grace. While the process was not perfect, this extraordinary manifestation of collective grace went a long way toward healing the deep racial rifts in that country.[19] The same spirit motivated the American civil rights movement in its use of nonviolent means to achieve racial justice.

But while we can find examples of the exercise of grace by a community, it is too often neglected in the making of public policy. Social-welfare-policy experts have long noted, for example, the often misplaced moralism underlying actual welfare programs that hold that poor people are undeserving, that they are poor because of their own choices or a lack of self-discipline, that they need to get out and work like everybody else. This common view may be accurate in some cases, but the attitude is entirely misguided in respect to children and all those who, by accident or circumstance, have been unable to provide adequately for themselves. A grace-informed welfare policy would seek to avoid judgmental attitudes, while helping to ensure that everybody has the means necessary to function in the community. When we ask whether poor people should be given what they need, the grace-filled answer is, Just do it. That, at least, should be the presumption.

Are there exceptions to such a grace-filled kind of public policy that can bear the burden of proof? There would be, I suppose, in any society that simply lacks the means to make generous provision for its poor people. That exception does not, of course, apply to the very wealthy countries of North America and Europe—or to Japan, Australia, New Zealand, and the rapidly developing countries of Asia.

Ironically, the burden of proof can be met if a too-generous provision of economic needs undermines the humanity of recipients. The U.S. welfare reform legislation in 1996, for example, was prompted by the view that too many welfare recipients who were capable of employment were not working. For their own sake, it was argued, they needed to be motivated to seek jobs, thereby improving their economic circumstances and gaining greater self-esteem. A case was made that the Aid to Families with Dependent Children program that was being revised had had the perverse effect of discouraging employment while also failing to provide adequate levels of subsistence for its recipients. Having studied this problem for several decades, I believed by 1996 that the argument was valid, although I also believed that the changes in the program were too sweeping: while denying benefits to force people to work, there was not enough effort to ensure that there were enough jobs for them. Society must make certain guarantees, this being one; the possibility of work should not simply be left to market forces, as it was.

Public school education may be a better example of what could be called grace at work in social policy. There are good, bad, and indifferent public schools. But common to all of them is the principle that if you are a child, you are eligible to receive an education at public expense, whether you "deserve" to or not. In fact, in each of the American states (and the District of Columbia) you are *required* to receive an education, either in the public schools or through private alternatives or home schooling.

2. A presumption for the value of each human life. The intrinsic value of every human being is deeply grounded in Christian faith. In Christian tradition the applicable metaphor is the *imago Dei*, the belief that we are created in the "image of God." The precise meaning of that term is subject to endless debate among theologians, but common to all is the profound sense that we are all valued by God, and this belief is underscored by the doctrine of grace, which we have already discussed. God's creation of human beings may have gotten flawed by human sin—which I discuss below—but still we are treated as persons of value. In any case, it is not a part of the job description of human beings to make ultimate judgments concerning the unworthiness of others. Actions we can, and often must, judge. Persons themselves are to be judged only by God, and fortunately for all of us, God's love overrides our flaws.

The value of each human life, treated as a presumption, means that we cannot treat other people as worthless trash or second-class citizens. No human cultural, racial, or national identity is as important as this fundamental assessment of everyone's value. No one should be defined fundamentally by those noteworthy but less important aspects of our lives, whether they are accidents of birth, the products of nurturing, or personal choices.

Such a presumption means that only for extreme reasons, such as protective police action, can we destroy human lives or treat anybody as *only* a means to our other ends. Immanuel Kant underscored this presumption in his famous declaration that there is an ethical imperative to treat other persons as ends in themselves, and not only as means. Obviously, we relate to one another also as means: We all use products and services that others supply. As passengers in an airplane or a bus, we don't think of pilot or driver principally as a person; rather, we relate to them through the necessary role they are playing in our safe transportation. Nevertheless, even as we "use" people in such a way, we treat them as persons whenever that is possible—or at least with a friendly greeting and smile when we leave the conveyance.

This presumption also argues for fairness in law and economic life. The legal right of habeas corpus, for example, guarantees that a person who has been arrested must receive full due process; it applies to prisoners of war as well and requires that they be treated appropriately and not mistreated, which certainly excludes torturing them. I am not aware of a burden of proof to the contrary ever being sufficiently weighty to set that presumption aside, despite arguments made to the contrary in light of, for example, the U.S. detention of political prisoners in Guantanamo.

Medical triage situations, in which choices about the treatment of patients must be made in the face of limited time and resources, can be particularly difficult. The burden might be at times reasonably met by giving higher priority to those who most need a scarce treatment and are most likely to benefit from it, but the burden of proof should be against selecting some persons as having greater intrinsic value than others. The problem becomes more difficult when judgments are made about which patients have the greatest value to the community. We should be reluctant to endorse that way of setting priorities, but perhaps a case can be made when a particular person, for instance, a national leader, would be better able to help others and therefore should have the best possible medical care, if a choice must be made. Still, the presumption has to be that each person has intrinsic value.

3. A presumption for the unity of humankind. We are made for relationship not only with God but also with one another. The family metaphor is appropriate: We are sisters and brothers in God's intended family of humankind. Therefore, forces and barriers turning people against fellow human beings must bear the burden of proof. That must be true at every level of human community, from the immediate family to the worldwide community. There are specific biblical teachings that underscore this point, such as Jesus' parable of the Good Samaritan and the remarkable second chapter of Ephesians, which speaks of Jesus' own importance as enabling reconciliation with God and breaking down "the dividing wall, that is, the hostility between us." The world, at every level, seems full of dividing walls. Some of these bespeak indifference to the value of persons of other groups; some are even lethal in their effects. But the presumption must be that we truly belong to one another and that dividing walls must bear the burden of proof. This isn't just good moral advice; it is an expression of our very nature as human beings. Aristotle observed that human beings are by nature social beings. We are of course individual as well, but individuality apart from community is unthinkable.

This presumption of human unity is constantly tested. Alienation within family units can be especially tragic; something of our very humanity is diminished by the conflicts separating us from those with whom we have had the deepest, most long-standing relationships. Such barriers range from the trivial to the huge and truly unsurmountable. But the presumption should be in favor of working at breaking down even the most difficult ones.

Of course, it is not possible to have intimate personal relationships with everybody on earth! Barriers of geography, nationality, and language are quite real. Even these barriers need not express human alienation, however. Wherever we are, we can find ways to communicate our fellow humanity with others. Some of the most tragic forms of alienation occur when law or custom disdains persons by reason of race or ethnicity or gender; against these the burden of proof should be clear and unrelenting. National boundaries create a different kind of dilemma. On the one hand, national boundaries are arbitrary divisions that should not be considered absolute. On the other hand, a national community is a kind of social unit, generally with common traditions and a single language or at least a limited number of languages. The dilemma is how to preserve the values of a shared national community without diminishing the broader commonality of the universal human family. Often this dilemma is heightened by economic disparities among nations, a subject to which I will return later.

4. A presumption for equality. It follows from the value of each human being and the presumption for unity, that all human beings should be considered equal. Many people question such a presumption, but does it not follow from belief in the intrinsic worth of each person? Within a political community, everyone must be equal before the law. Similarly, within a family each member is considered to be equal—and every parent knows how closely that presumption of equality is monitored by their offspring! Despite the presumption, many exceptions can be justified, even for the sake of preserving or restoring equality itself. For example, consider a family with two children, one of whom has an early need for eyeglasses, the other for corrective surgery. In both cases, what is needed by one is not needed by the other, and the exceptional treatment is required to restore equality. If the medical conditions were reversed, the treatment would also be reversed. Such exceptions are need-driven, not favoritism. Even equality before the law must be amenable to the use of both positive and negative legal incentives—rewards and punishments. Still, economic and educational policies should operate with the presumption of equality and with inequalities of treatment required to bear the burden of proof.

5. A presumption for preferential claims for the poor and marginalized. Latin American liberation theology has asserted a faith-based "preferential option for the poor," that we should give highest priority to meeting the needs and aspirations of poor people. That preferential option is not at all hard to defend biblically; throughout the Bible we find repeated references to God's love for the poor and the obligation of their economically more fortunate neighbors to serve them. But this priority is also logical: Poor people are the point at which the unity of the community is most vulnerable; they are, so to speak, the weakest link in the chain. It is not that poor people are necessarily morally better than the more fortunate—although they often may be; it is that we all suffer from the fragmentation of community and should do what it takes to avoid that.

Perhaps there should also be a preferential regard for other kinds of marginalized people, especially those who have been stigmatized by virtue of racial or ethnic status, gender, sexual orientation, age, illness, or some other defining characteristic that is seen as more important than their essential humanity. Jesus' concern for the marginalized and stigmatized people of his time is striking, and it may have been an important part of what got him into really serious trouble!

For the past thirty years or so, American society has struggled over what came to be called affirmative action. In brief, affirmative action policies give special consideration to persons whose racial, ethnic, or gender identity has historically been a major liability. This meant providing special opportunity for African Americans, Asian Americans, and women seeking admission to educational institutions, employment in businesses and governmental agencies, and leadership positions in churches. Opponents of affirmative action argue that the policy denies equal opportunity for all persons. Supporters argue that, in the race of life, previous inequalities have created uneven starting points. For example, to be African American is to be a part of a historic category of persons whose older ancestors were slaves and whose more recent forebears suffered the humiliations and disadvantages of racial discrimination and institutional segregation. That legacy affects a person's ability to compete as an equal with persons who have not had that disadvantage. Moreover, supporters of affirmative action assert that institutions deprived of visible diversity are thereby weakened; having students and professors with different backgrounds is in itself an educational value for everybody, not just for those who have been included through affirmative action.

If we treat affirmative action as a presumption, we must remember that it is counterproductive to put people in positions where they are bound to fail. Affirmative action cannot, therefore, be a simple matter of meeting quotas, without considering a person's qualifications or abilities, for that would be demeaning to persons of genuine ability, whose participation or leadership is discounted. Still, the presumption can lean toward greater inclusiveness, and, where needed, special programs can and should be developed to help overcome legacies of disability.

It can be quite difficult to know when programs like affirmative action have run their course and are no longer needed. But let's take a clear example. For many years, African Americans were totally excluded from participation in professional sports in this country, except for the specifically African American baseball leagues, which were looked down upon by the white majority. A few venturesome steps were taken—one thinks especially of Jackie Robinson becoming the first major league baseball player. In the beginning, the handful of athletes breaking the color barrier had to be exceptionally good and willing to put up with terrible pressures. Today, that is no longer the case with professional or intercollegiate athletics. No affirmative action is needed to ensure the presence of African American or Latino athletes in major league baseball, the National Football League, or the National Basketball Association. They are present in large numbers, and their performance is outstanding. While this success was not due to affirmative action, the initial inclusion of African American athletes *was* a result of deliberate decisions made in the face of considerable opposition. For instance, Branch Rickey's inclusion of Jackie Robinson was deliberate, well thought out, and undertaken despite immense public resistance.

Gradually, broad inclusiveness seems to be happening in other areas of life as well, such as churches, businesses, and public service. This is not yet a perfectly inclusive society, however, and the need for affirmative action is not over. I suppose we can say that the presumption for affirmative action can be set aside when those who have previously needed such assistance are clearly valued for their own sake as individuals. We may differ in our assessments of when that time has come, but if we keep faith with the principle of full inclusion, there will come a time when it is obvious to most people that further affirmative action is not needed.

6. A presumption for the goodness of creation. The conservation of nature as it is or once was cannot be an absolute. Human civilization has from the beginning developed by means of the conquest of nature—bending it, so to speak, toward human ends. Still, a Christian perspective on nature (paralleled in a number of other religions) is that it has a worth beyond its usefulness to people. The first chapter of Genesis underscores this, as after each aspect of the natural world, God is represented as seeing "that it was good." Nature is depicted as giving God pleasure. Humanity, in this simple but profound characterization of creation, has the responsibility of nurturing nature, not running over it roughshod.

One of the earliest Christian heresies was the belief that the physical creation was not created by God—that we are essentially spirits, only encumbered by the physical. Very early

Christian docetism took that view, proclaiming that Jesus Christ was essentially spiritual and only appeared to be physical. But how are we to function in our physical bodies in a very physical world, if that world's reality is thus to be questioned? The biblical alternative is to consider the natural world, including the physical aspects of our own being, as created by God and thus expressing divine purpose.

In chapters 7 and 8, I discuss the hard choices that must be made about the environment, but for now it is enough to say that two views in particular must be *excluded* from any theological consideration: (1) the notion that the natural world is simply there for human exploitation; (2) the negative attitude toward everything physical, either as source of evil or as unreal. We are spiritual beings, to be sure. But we occupy physical bodies in a physical universe that is to be understood as good, not only for us but for God.

THE LIMITS AND FLAWS IN HUMAN NATURE

The moral presumptions we have discussed thus far represent the positive values that are grounded in the benevolent purposes of God and the fundamental purposes of the moral life. We must now consider our limitations and how we must take them into account in our decision-making. Our presumption must be *against* anybody's being considered to be all-knowing or perfectly good.

1. **A presumption of human limitations.** The first of these presumptions is obvious. I've already commented upon our limitations as human beings—our limited intelligence, knowledge, experience, judgment. We are not God; we are very far from having the whole picture. Quite apart from any moral failings, we cannot pretend to intellectual perfection. That is not because we are bad people; it is simply the truth about our creaturely condition as human beings. This presumption protects our moral judgments from being overly impressed by

human expertise and authority. We all must rely upon experts of various kinds, and we give the benefit of the doubt to persons having positions of authority. But this presumption of human limitation can save us from absolute, unquestioning reliance upon the experts and authorities. We must take into account that they may be wrong. So, to put this in a complicated way, we may presume that the experts and authorities are right, but we take into account that they may be wrong. Practically speaking, we do not grant experts and authorities unlimited power over our individual lives or over society.

For instance, I have great respect for doctors. Confronted by a physical health problem, I will seek out the best available medical advice, and I will tend to do what I am advised to do. But, often enough, I have experienced the limitations of the medical profession. I think most doctors are quite good, but they are not perfect. I have known instances, both personally and as a pastor, when good doctors made mistakes. So in my mind they enjoy the presumption of being right, but not an absolute conviction that they are. Sometimes one falls back upon contrary personal experience; sometimes one seeks a second opinion. As another illustration, papal infallibility may be the strongest religious statement of the absolute rightness of judgment rendered by a human being in authority. But, if I understand the status of that Roman Catholic view, teaching that is to be considered infallible has been limited to two or three instances in more than a hundred years. Most papal teaching, including the many twentieth-century papal encyclicals, is taken to have very high authority, but is not regarded as absolute. One could say that popes are presumed to be right, with a heavy burden of proof to be borne by those who venture to disagree. The pope, while the most authoritative figure in that church, is not considered to be God. He doesn't know everything; he can be mistaken. But the view of that church is that he usually is right.

2. A presumption against anyone's moral perfection. We are sinners who fall short of even our own conception of the good.

That, too, is undeniable truth, and it's exaggerated by our sinful tendency toward self-justification. Among the many accounts of the much-debated Christian doctrine of original sin, the one I find most persuasive is Reinhold Niebuhr's in *The Nature and Destiny of Man*. Niebuhr speaks of sin as not necessary but inevitable. It is not necessary because we retain moral freedom; it is inevitable because of the internal human dynamics that lead us toward self-centeredness. Defining original sin, the basic condition of sinfulness, as pride, Niebuhr notes that while we comprehend the realities of universal space and time, we are also aware of our own finitude. We are going to die, and we know it. So we seek a universal meaning for ourselves by placing ourselves at the center of this vast universe:

> Man is insecure and involved in natural contingency; he seeks to overcome his insecurity by a will-to-power which overreaches the limits of human creatureliness. Man is ignorant and involved in the limitations of a finite mind; but he pretends that he is not limited. He assumes that he can gradually transcend finite limitations until his mind becomes identical with universal mind. All of his intellectual and cultural pursuits, therefore, become infected with the sin of pride. . . . Even when sin is expressed as sensuality, that also betrays some aspect of his abortive effort to solve the problem of finiteness and freedom.[20]

Because all human beings are thus limited morally, we cannot presume that anybody is altogether wise or good. The presumption that emerges instead is *against* anybody's perfection—or any group's perfection, for that matter.

In his moral case for democracy, Niebuhr relies on that insight in part: "Man's capacity for justice makes democracy possible; but man's inclination to injustice makes democracy necessary."[21] Nobody can be trusted with absolute power. Obviously we have to trust one another in the exercise of power, but the presumption of human imperfection, or limitation, is a deep reason for holding power accountable by means of various checks and balances of different branches of government, by periodic elections, and by an independent judiciary. The judiciary, although important in sustaining human rights against oppressive majorities, must itself also be held accountable. These forms of accountability provide an intricate blend of forces and authorities in a democratic society. The presumption of human limitation is important in maintaining that blend creatively.

3. A presumption against self-interest. A third presumption is against our own self-interest when it is in conflict with the interests of others. We all have a tendency to look out for ourselves first and foremost. That is common and sometimes quite appropriate. But the very fact of its commonness should lead us to question more deeply its appropriateness. Who, within the inner forum of our conscience, is going to represent that one whose interests are in conflict with our own? Should we not counter our own tendencies toward selfishness by forcing our own self-interest to bear the burden of the proof?

An illustration of how this might work: Consider the biblical provision for tithing—giving away a tenth of our income to religious bodies or causes more directly expressing, as far as we can discern, the purposes of God. Taking that much of our income "off the top," so to speak, is one way of implementing a presumption against our own immediate self-interest. Wealthier people should do much more; poor people can meet the burden of proof by doing much less. Indeed, exceptions to the presumption against one's self-interest can readily be justified when that self-interest corresponds to that of an oppressed people. We should not object when women or members of racial minorities seek to overcome historic barriers, even when it is in their own personal self-interest to do so. It is, rather, the maintaining of such barriers that should bear the burden of proof! At the same time, persons who belong to groups that have suffered oppression also must be sensitive to their own limitations and to the legitimate needs of *other* oppressed groups. Moral decision-making is complex!

In suggesting a presumption against our own self-interest, I am not suggesting that we burden ourselves with guilt. We are all assuredly sinners. But that does not mean (to reverse the famous quotation from Jonathan Edwards) that we are in the hands of an angry God. The point of moving away from self-interest is, rather, figuring out how to express love realistically. To be realistic is to weigh one's natural tendency toward self-interest and to compensate for it by creating a presumption against it. Often the presumption can be set aside, for many of our interests are not necessarily selfish. But people with a deep sense of their limitations will in doubtful cases give the benefit of the doubt to the worthy interests of others.

PRESUMPTIONS THAT PRESERVE BALANCE

To tease the imagination some more, there are *balances* that must be preserved in our moral decision-making. The philosopher Aristotle observed that good judgment is likely to be found in the "golden mean" between excess and deficiency. Sometimes our choices confront us with opposites that must both be preserved if we are to remain faithful to the deeper insights of our faith traditions. If one side or the other of these opposites is abandoned, the effect is to undermine both sides. It is almost like children on a playground seesaw: remove either child, and it is no longer possible to use the seesaw. I will mention three of these opposites that are basic to ethics. Many more could also be suggested, but these three are especially important.

1. Sin vs. goodness in human nature. The presumption of human limitation and sinfulness must in the end be balanced by due regard for the goodness that is also in human nature. The theological affirmation that we are born with the "image of God" (the *imago Dei*) means that there is something good in us from the start. Even though original sin distorts our natural goodness, and even though some theologies hold that the fall and sin have eradicated the image of God from us, such total pessimism cannot be sustained biblically or practically. Biblically, there are just too many accounts of people who were morally upright, even without the benefit of having been "saved" by Jesus Christ. What

about Moses, and Ruth, and Uriah, and Esther? The widow in
the temple? Characters in some of Jesus' own parables, such as
the good Samaritan and the father of the prodigal son? And practically, we all have known or known about people who may not
have been Christian but who are or were very good.

Among the good non-Christian people are untold millions
of mothers, worldwide, lovingly nurturing their children; generous benefactors of the poor; non-Christian public servants,
wisely caring for the common good; even many atheistic Marx-
ists, confused though they may have been, who were unselfishly
devoted to the good as they understood it. I learned this lesson
personally in 1975 during the Cold War, when my family was
traveling by VW bus from Berlin to Prague. At the border
between Communist East Germany and Communist Czecho-
slovakia, we experienced car trouble while waiting in a long line
of çars heading toward Prague. Everybody, including the presumably Communist officials at the border crossing, was more
than helpful, even though we were obviously Americans, considered their enemies in the Cold War. We learned that day, as
we had on other occasions, never to assume hostility in a strange
setting from strangers. At some level, we are apt to experience
anew our common humanity.

Does this acknowledgment of non-Christian persons of
laudable moral character set aside the presumption of sinfulness? Of course not. But it requires us to balance that presumption with one in favor of goodness in other people. As
Niebuhr's aphorism reminds us, democracy is made possible by
the human capacity for justice, just as it is made necessary by
the human inclination toward injustice. We don't have to arrive
at a precise balancing of the two. No doubt, the balance fluctu-
ates within and between different people.

2. Free will vs. determinism. A similarly imprecise balance exists
within all of us between our personal moral freedom and the
forces that consciously or unconsciously determine our actions.
Every biblical admonition to act in accordance with God's gift of
love and to avoid evil presupposes that we are at least somewhat

free to respond to that charge. But at the same time, our freedom is constrained by forces we cannot control. How great is that constraint? We cannot say precisely, but we do know that both are involved in all of us. Freedom could not exist without some determinism—for without some determinism in the exercise of our freedom we could not determine anything about the future. But determinism is logically impossible as well. For, if everything about us is determined, how could we even know that? Theologian Paul Tillich refers to this polarity as being between freedom and destiny, destiny meaning everything that bears upon us to determine our future, and freedom meaning our capacity to help shape that future. How do we translate this polarity into a moral presumption? It can at least mean that we should never presume that other people are simply and entirely determined by their environment, their upbringing, or forces bearing upon them. The presumption is, rather, that people are responsible beings and should be treated as such. On the other hand, we should never presume that those forces shaping our destiny are unimportant. How, for instance, are we to shape actions and policies to help liberate people from poverty? If we presume that the poor are personally responsible for their plight, we miss all of the negative conditions that have in large measure led them to where they are. These can include a dysfunctional family background, perhaps dating back several generations, as well as inadequate educational opportunity, street violence, physical or sexual abuse, inadequate health care and nutrition, negative stereotyping and discrimination in the wider community. Such forces are often very real, and to ignore them is to be quite unrealistic. On the other hand, to treat anybody as *nothing more* than the end result of the negative influences is to dehumanize that person. That, too, is unrealistic, for everybody has *some* degree of freedom to work with. Usually, though, that germ of moral freedom is greatly enhanced by caring personal relationships and supportive economic and social conditions.

So we can refer to this relationship between freedom and determinism as a polar presumption. The presumption is that everybody is both a free agent and the product of determining forces. The burden of proof must be borne by those who treat people as *entirely* one or the other. As we shall see, this polar presumption bears upon criminal law and economic policy.

3. Optimism vs. pessimism. Yet another polar presumption, deeply grounded in Christian faith, is between the hopeful attitude that good can result from human action and the recognition that the good we seek will never be fully possible in a world of finite limitations and persistent sin. Eschatology is the part of Christian theology that considers how human history will reach its consummation in the final victory of God. The book of Revelation is the most striking biblical expression of eschatology, although the theme is also found elsewhere in the Bible, such as parts of Isaiah, Daniel, Matthew, and 1 Corinthians. Theologians have at times so emphasized God's definitive role in the end time that human efforts and partial moral victories in the meantime have been severely discounted. In practice, this can lead to a hopeless attitude about the world and the loss of motivation to seek needed change. Placing everything in God's hands overlooks or ignores the extent to which God has placed things in *our* hands!

How often do pessimists affect human history? Doesn't a more hopeful attitude, even if somewhat unrealistic, often make a difference? Small groups of people infused with hope have achieved extraordinary results. The American civil rights revolution was initially led by a relatively small number of venturesome people who, in Martin Luther King Jr.'s memorable phrase, "had a dream." About the time this dream was taking shape in the Montgomery bus boycott in the 1950s, a book appeared with the title *The Deep South Says NEVER*.[22] Written by John Bartlow Martin, the book dealt with the deep opposition among southern whites to the 1954 Supreme Court decision that racial segregation in public schools was unconstitutional. "Never" proved to be a considerable overestimate of the length of time required for desegregation to arrive throughout the South, although other factors have, to this day, made the achievement of full integration elusive.

Changes like this do not occur automatically, in the midst of passive onlookers. Social reform takes resolute action by committed people who are prepared to suffer abuse in the process. But who could say that injustices have never been dealt with successfully? We *can* say with certainty, however, that actions to change history are much more successful when mounted by people who believe they can be successful. The late Raymond Wilson, longtime leader of the Washington-based Friends Committee on National Legislation, often said that great legislative reforms take twenty years to accomplish. My own involvements and observations in the nation's capital suggest that sometimes it takes a good deal longer than that! Surely that means that optimism about the possibility of change must be accompanied by patience, even a willingness to accept the fact that we ourselves may never see the results of our efforts.

Even while optimistic, we must recognize that in the end perfection will ever be beyond our grasp. The conventional eschatological formula speaks of the coming of God's realm on earth as "already, but not yet." On earth, inspired by hope, we can accomplish much. God is already present, and divine purposes have been gained. But on earth, more will always remain beyond human grasp.

This presumption holds to that tension. It is a presumption against hopelessness, on the one hand, and against utopia, on the other. A burden of proof should have to be borne by those who argue that a needed social improvement (or an individual's transformation, for that matter) is impossible. It should also have to be borne by those who promise that their proposal will bring social or individual perfection. When perfect utopias are dangled before us, we are well reminded that insistence on perfection can be an obstacle to the achievement of the possible good.

A PRESUMPTION FOR SCRIPTURE AND TRADITION

We have already briefly noted both the limitations in taking biblical moral teachings literally and absolutely and the shortcomings of some long-standing historical traditions. However, given the formative importance of Scripture and tradition (and bearing in mind that the Bible is itself the foundational part of tradition), we should be prepared to grant a presumption for this legacy that has been so important in making us Christians who we are.

By this I mean that among Christians the burden of proof should be borne by those who find it necessary to deviate from the Bible and tradition. In not a few cases, that burden is easily borne. Often, in fact, one objectionable aspect of biblical teaching or of tradition is corrected by other parts. Jesus himself calls attention to that: "You have heard it said, but I say unto you." If the true authority of the Bible is derived from the leading of the Holy Spirit, then who are we to say that the Holy Spirit, having already done the biblical thing, is no longer active to help correct what biblical writers only mistakenly considered to be inspired? It is quite obvious to objective readers that parts of the Bible express dated cultural influences and that the deeper currents of biblical faith require correction. But while the burden of proof can often be met, we do well to observe the presumption.

WHEN PRESUMPTIONS ARE IN CONFLICT

In addressing the hard moral questions, thinking more clearly about our moral presumptions is useful, but does not always yield clear answers. One reason is that sometimes different good presumptions can lead in opposite directions. For instance, a presumption in favor of lifting people out of poverty, which can lead to emphasizing economic development, conflicts with a presumption in favor of environmental conservation, which can lead to a de-emphasis on economic development. A presumption in favor of life is in conflict with a presumption for freedom, in the case of laws relating to abortion. And then there are clear conflicts between the Bible and tradition, on the one hand, and various positive presumptions we have discussed in this chapter. There is no overarching theological presumption that will provide indisputable answers.

Except this one: Every particular presumption must yield to the deeper faith that is the underlying basis for all of them—just as all presumptions must confront their consequences in the factual world. This is yet another reminder that, even with settled convictions and firm commitments, we remain open to new truth and to insights gained in conversation with others. In the discussion of some of the "hard choices" facing all people of goodwill in the twenty-first century, that combination of conviction and openness must be sustained. I believe the approach described in this book can serve us well: clarifying our presumptions, with the openness to consider whether a contrary burden of proof has been met.

PART 2

Applications and Illustrations

6

Difficult Personal Decisions

Personal and communal decisions are intertwined. In our personal choices we are often greatly influenced by the wider community. And collective decisions, made by the community as a whole, are in many ways an aggregate expression of the personal choices of its individual members. Still, a distinction can be made between these two levels of decision-making. Personal choices are not determined or required by the wider community, despite whatever influences the community may exert upon us. And community decisions can be, and often are, made despite the opposition of many individuals.

In this chapter we consider the personal decisions. We confront them all the time. We can get a useful reminder of the range of such decisions by reading newspaper advice columns like "Dear Abby" or the Sunday *New York Times Magazine*'s ethics column. Some of the personal problems aired in such places are trivial, some of the advice may not seem terribly wise, and some truly important personal dilemmas are rarely encountered. Nevertheless, most of the problems posed involve moral choices. In what follows, I consider some of the typical hard choices we confront in our personal lives. (I will not, here, be referring to the advice columns!)

SEXUAL INTIMACY AND FAMILY LIFE

Some of the most delicate and difficult human decisions relate to sex. The subject of sex has caused all kinds of grief through Christian history, and has often been accompanied by the sense that sexual expression is somehow morally questionable. Augustine is partly to blame for this by relating original sin to human sexuality, and Paul's writings suggest that it's better to avoid sex if it's at all possible. In fact, for much of its history, the Christian church has come close to saying that asceticism is the holiest form of life.

It is easy to overstate such views, of course, but that historical legacy has reached down to the present time and continues to color attitudes in our time. Yet a negative view of sex is quite contrary to the general Christian presumption of the goodness of created existence. The burden of proof must be borne by any conclusion that sexual expression is intrinsically sinful. To be human is, at least for a vast majority, to be a sexual being; Christian churches increasingly recognize that. In a declaration typical of this attitude, the United Methodist Church has declared that "we recognize that sexuality is God's good gift to all persons. We believe persons may be fully human only when that gift is acknowledged and affirmed by themselves, the church, and society. We call all persons to the disciplined, responsible fulfillment of themselves, others, and society in the stewardship of this gift."[23]

So why have Christians ever considered sexual expression to be questionable? That is a very complex question, and I doubt whether any of us can give a complete answer. Perhaps it is in part because sex is such a powerful sensual force that it can come to dominate one's life, so that it becomes more difficult to center that life on God. In traditional theological language, this is called idolatry. Perhaps people have difficulty with sex because of the dehumanizing character of sexual exploitation and abuse. When other persons are reduced to being only sexual objects, the humanity of both the abused and the abuser is diminished. When we dehumanize others, we dehumanize ourselves. The sexual abuse of children, sexual assault, and spousal abuse are great human tragedies. Not infrequently, those who commit such abuses have themselves been abused and thus perpetuate the tragedies from one generation to the next. There must be no uncertainty about our rejection of such abuses, and programs designed to prevent and to heal deserve our full support.

But the fact of sexual abuse is not a reason to consider sexual expression to be sinful. It may push us, however, to consider more deeply how sexual expression can enhance, not diminish, humanizing relationships. When the intensity of sex is combined with the commitment of love, the result can be a new wholeness. Biblical language, incorporated into religious wedding ceremonies, speaks of such relationships as covenantal. A covenant, such as the covenant of marriage, is much more than a contract. Beyond any legal or legalistic connotations, it is a commitment in love of two persons to one another.

Some comment must be made about a striking new wrinkle in North America and Europe related to such covenants. Early in the twenty-first century, very large numbers of people are involved in what could be called premarital, semicommitted sexual relationships. At least these are semicommitted in comparison with the lifelong commitment ("until death us do part") that is formalized in a wedding ceremony. If a couple is living together as a way of testing whether a more lasting marriage covenant would work out, that relationship can be called a trial marriage. The percentage may vary regionally to some extent, but anecdotal evidence shared among clergy now suggests that as many as 80 or 90 percent of couples at whose weddings they have officiated were living together prior to marriage.

Two questions emerge from this trend: First, what is the character of the premarital relationship itself? If the relationship is in fact tentative, what is the effect of this tentativeness upon the humanizing values? Second, when such relationships do lead to marriage, is the marriage more or less likely to succeed? Since satisfactory answers to these important questions cannot yet be given, this can still be considered a kind of large-scale experiment. But no matter what it is, this cultural trend won't just go away. If such relationships are in fact more humanizing and more likely to lead to successful marriages, then we can expect this widespread tendency to enter more permanently into the culture. Otherwise, it will gradually fade away. In the language of moral presumption, there is a fairly strong presumption in Christian tradition against such relationships. Perhaps what is now being tested is whether there are sufficient grounds to set that presumption aside.

Most of these observations can readily be applied to the tangled issue of homosexuality. I will deal with this as a public policy issue in the next chapter, but here it can be said that homosexual relationships should also be governed by the standard of covenantal love if they are to be fully humanizing. Out of my own pastoral experience, and as a result of conversation with other pastors, I can affirm that many gay and lesbian couples exemplify the humanizing reality of covenantal love.

CONTRACEPTION AND ABORTION

The widespread use of artificial methods of birth control is, historically, a fairly recent phenomenon. Less than a century ago, contraception was much less accepted than it is today. The strongest statement against what is today a very common practice in much of the world came in the 1930 encyclical of the Roman Catholic Pope Pius XI, *Casti Connubii*: "Since, therefore, the conjugal act is destined primarily by nature for the begetting of children, those who in exercising it deliberately frustrate its natural power and purpose sin against nature and commit a deed which is shameful and intrinsically vicious."

While the language was softened in Pope Paul VI's encyclical *Humanae Vitae* of 1968, the essential teaching remained the same: contraception is contrary to nature and must, therefore, be considered sinful. This conclusion too has been subject to widespread social change, and today most Christians no longer consider the religious teaching against contraception to be morally binding.

The contrary conclusion, affirmed also to some extent by papal teaching, is that the sex act in marriage can be very humanizing, quite apart from the begetting of children. One could almost reverse the negative attitude toward contraception by saying that there is a moral presumption in favor of responsible family planning. What then is the right number of children for a family? Surely the answer will vary according to different personal and social situations. But as a general proposition, should it not be a number consistent with each child's being loved wholeheartedly and nurtured in such a way that the child's potential can be realized?

A woman with an unwanted or physically dangerous pregnancy faces one of the most agonizing decisions a person can have: whether to have an abortion. The question of abortion is much more complicated than the issue of contraception, and contemporary attitudes remain quite divided. Postponing until the next chapter the question whether abortion should be prohibited by law, there is much to be said for a presumption that a pregnancy should not be terminated. Many Christians, including especially many Roman Catholics and Protestant evangelicals, wish to make this an absolute, thus treating abortion as always wrong. The basis for this is the view that human life, from the moment of conception, is to be invested with the full value of each human being after birth. The *imago Dei*, so to speak, is present from that first moment. That is not a judgment that can be proven factually. But neither can it be established factually that *anybody* possesses the *imago Dei*! That is an article of faith, sustained in this case by the fact that earliest embryonic life will, unless terminated by abortion or natural miscarriage, develop in a seamless process to be born as an infant.

The case against abortion, seen in that perspective, is no different from the case against infanticide, and most of us would treat rejection of infanticide not as a presumption but as an absolute, or at least a near absolute. For those who do not accept the idea that abortion is wrong during the early stages of pregnancy—much less at the very beginning, when only a handful of cells is involved—the rejection of abortion may be more on the level of presumption. Given the potentiality of a particular pregnancy developing into full human life, the presumption can very well be against abortion. But are there circumstances, in the early stages, that would meet the burden of proof? Answers vary, depending on the individual circumstances, even among those who accept the morality of abortion in some situations. For example, what if the pregnant woman is so young—say, a twelve-year-old—she cannot even be considered a woman? What if the pregnancy is the result of rape or incest, so that the child would be a living reminder of severe trauma? Would the pregnancy, carried to term, destroy other important life prospects for a young woman? Is the family so hard pressed economically that an additional child would severely diminish the development of children who are already present? Carried to term, would the child be unwanted and unloved? Would continuation of the pregnancy be injurious to the health or even the life of the mother? In a situation where contraception failure has frustrated the intention of responsible parenthood, does the fact of pregnancy entirely set aside the moral validity of that intention?

These are not trivial questions, and they will be answered in different ways by different people. But as a matter of personal choice, by those most immediately affected, the presumption is in favor of continuing a pregnancy. When contemplating a possible abortion, those facing the decision—and those whose counsel is being sought—should weigh carefully whether there are sufficient grounds to set the presumption aside. But to make an absolute out of that presumption is to set aside morally weighty grounds for choosing abortion in some circumstances. In the next chapter, we will consider whether abortion should be prohibited or otherwise regulated by law. But abortion is always a hard choice for individuals facing what appear to be intolerable consequences if a pregnancy is allowed to continue—even when it is prohibited by law.

A related but somewhat different decision—use of the "morning-after pill" to prevent a pregnancy following sexual intercourse—may be less fraught with difficulty, despite the fact that some people consider it the equivalent of abortion. Similarly, opposition to stem-cell research, on the questionable grounds that the stem cell could become a person, fails to take into account the great potential benefits of such research in conquering serious diseases. I am among those who would not treat opposition to the pill or stem-cell research as a moral presumption. I would rather argue that the burden of proof should be borne by those who oppose either.

But to take the issue perhaps to its logical extreme: Is there any theological basis for believing that every conceivable (pun intended) life should be created? It might appear so, since life is so good, and every human being is understood theologically to bear the *imago Dei*. But it would in short order prove to be literally a disaster if all women had as many children as they were capable of having. Worldwide, most families would quickly be stretched beyond their means, and unrestrained population growth would tax every nation's economic resources and environmental balances severely. To put the issue theologically, God has created a limited world. To put it practically, when population expands without restraint, it is in due course checked by the ancient enemies of disease and famine. Responsible planning, both in the microcosm of a family unit and in the larger scale of whole societies, is essential to humankind's fulfilling the divine purposes of creation.

CHOOSING A SPOUSE

In a typical Christian wedding ceremony, bride and groom are asked to commit themselves to each other in lifelong union, "until death us do part." Some wedding liturgies also refer to the curious analogy that marriage reflects Christ's relationship with his church. According to some interpretations, this means that as Christ is head of the church, the husband is head of the wife. Perhaps that was what was originally intended by those who developed this liturgy. I do not know. But such an interpretation misses the deeper point: If Christ is understood to be the expression of God's grace to the church, then *both* spouses (or gay and lesbian partners) can be seen as manifestations of that grace to one another. So, if God's grace is that unconditional love of God for flawed humanity, despite our undeserving nature, spouses are in commitment to express unconditional love to each other. Since neither husband nor wife is Christ, it is a very difficult challenge for all of us in our humanity to express that kind of grace to one another!

In any case, the decision to commit oneself to another in this way is indescribably important. What can we say about that "hard choice"?

It is a bit difficult to frame this question on the basis of a moral presumption, as we have been using that term. Still, some negative presumptions about choice of a spouse may be in order. For instance, one should presume against making a lifetime commitment to another person for the sake of money or other forms of material security, or just in order to escape from a painful environment. This presumption should not be an absolute. Although we can think of extreme circumstances that might meet a burden of proof, the burden of proof should certainly be against it. Nor should one make the commitment to marry on the assumption that it will be possible to change serious flaws in a person who simply is not ready for marriage or who in other ways would be difficult to live with in the intimate covenant of marriage. It may be possible to facilitate change, but the odds are against it. One should also presume against a lifelong union with a person who is not prepared to enter into it as a covenant of equal respect.

These points, though negative, are fairly obvious. More positively, we should choose somebody who has also chosen us! To be affirmed wholeheartedly is a wonderfully humanizing thing. Being in such a union of mutual grace, undergirded by dependable lifetime commitment, is probably more important than more superficial similarities or differences. We have all seen highly successful unions of people who were very similar in skills, tastes, and life experience—and equally successful unions of people who have brought complementary, but quite different, gifts to each other. While the choice of a spouse is undeniably personal, it is also a part of a larger social matrix and needs the support of friends and loved ones who know both prospective spouses well enough to react wisely to the prospect. Although the presence of support should not be an absolute criterion, it should be considered seriously.

In the end, while choosing a spouse is a very important life decision, we cannot anticipate everything that the years will bring. So one must ask, is there every reason to believe that we can grow together as we experience life together through the years to come? Are we prepared to make that commitment "for better or worse, for richer or poorer, in sickness and health," trusting that we will really be there for each other, regardless?

DIVORCE

We are not perfect in our humanity. We can speak of marriage as the relationship between Christ and his church, but have no illusions that any of us are close to being like Christ or any of the other remarkable moral heroes we can name. Still, everything I've said so far about marriage establishes a very clear presumption in favor of keeping faith with the commitment. Divorce should have to bear a steep burden of proof.

For centuries, churches held in favor of marriage, not as a presumption but as an absolute. Divorced people could not be remarried with the blessing of the church. As I write these words, that remains the standard held by the Roman Catholic Church, although that denomination has so loosely administered the acceptable option of annulment as almost to accept divorce itself. When I became an ordained Methodist minister half a century ago, the denomination no longer absolutely prohibited the remarriage of divorced persons. Instead, it charged its clergy to ascertain whether a divorced person had been the party at fault in the divorce. This provision strikes most of us today as almost bizarre in light of the complex realities usually involved in divorce, and the provision was dropped years ago.[24] Still, in arriving at the hard and painful choice of divorce, there should be a serious presumption in favor of repairing and continuing the marriage. What are the circumstances that could meet the burden of proof against divorce? From the moral standpoint, this question could be framed along the lines of the classical criteria of a just (or justified) war. Depending on the formulation of just-war theory, there are some seven conditions that must be met before a Christian can approve of or participate in a war. Can we develop similar criteria to consider when contemplating divorce—either as one who is directly involved or as a counselor attempting to give wise counsel?

Ethicist Margaret A. Farley, while making it clear that a strong presumption for the preservation of a marriage must remain in place, suggests that there are three general conditions under which divorce may be defensible:

> A commitment no longer binds when (1) it becomes *impossible* to keep; (2) it no longer fulfills any of the *purposes* it was meant to serve; (3) another obligation comes into *conflict* with the first obligation, and the second is judged to override the first. Only one of these conditions needs to be in place—although often more than one characterizes the situation—in order to justify a release from the commitment-obligation.[25]

Professor Farley's thoughtful suggestions are an invitation to a further discussion about the conditions that might justify divorce.

I propose a list of somewhat more specific conditions that might justify divorce, trusting that others will continue this conversation. Faced with the reality of a painful marriage, people may find it very difficult to use these suggestions as a rational checklist to guide their thinking. Thinking about what conditions justify the breaking of the covenantal bond of marriage may be easier for counselors and friends who can be in a position to advise and offer support. When any of the following conditions are present, there are serious grounds for considering divorce:

1. One person has broken the covenant of mutual commitment and love so that it seems beyond repair. Sexual infidelity can be very painful, although many counselors will testify that some couples have been able to work successfully through the issue of sexual unfaithfulness and their marriage has been restored with integrity. Spousal abuse is, to some minds, even more of a problem. Where one party has begun to abuse the other physically or with ridicule, that cannot be tolerated. Obviously, when one party or the other has abandoned the marriage, that would meet the burden of proof.

2. Serious attempts at remediation have been made. In particular, counseling in good faith has been attempted, with a counselor who is committed, in general, to repairing troubled marriages and proposing divorce only when that is not possible. But this has not been successful.

3. The children of the marriage, if any, are more likely to be damaged by the continuation of the marriage than by its dissolution. Similarly, the example set by this divorce will not diminish the stability of other marriages in the circle of friendship or the wider community.

4. Friends and relatives who are intimately familiar with the couple consider a divorce to be a wise decision.

5. The initial decision to enter into the marriage in the first place was so very immature that growth toward mutual maturity is virtually impossible.

6. Sufficient time has elapsed, possibly with a trial separation, to indicate that the problems are simply too deep to surmount. (When difficulties in a marriage are worked through, it is not unusual for the relationship to become healthier than before.)

7. A new life can be constructed that will be better than life in the dysfunctional marriage. In contemplating the extreme measure of divorce, there is also a moral

responsibility for the continued well-being of the other person insofar as this is possible.

I want to emphasize again that the first criterion, above, is very important—particularly the point about physical abuse and ridicule. In heterosexual marriages, the woman is more likely to face that than her husband. Often the husband's push for dominance, even to the point of physically abusing and belittling his wife, is evidence of his own insecurity. The right kinds of therapeutic intervention can sometimes be successful, but a continued pattern of abuse should not be tolerated.

As we gain more experience with gay and lesbian unions, it seems evident that many endure through the years without such problems. That is all the more remarkable, given the overall lack of social and legal support such unions have. But when gay and lesbian unions become troubled, the reality may not be all that different from heterosexual marriages. And before dissolving the union, a gay or lesbian couple might also make the hard choice with a presumption in favor of continuing it and with an eye toward criteria suggested above.

VOCATIONAL CHOICES

Young people in our society, and increasingly older people as well, confront the big choice of vocational direction. The word *vocation*, derived from the Latin *vocare*, refers to a "calling," originally a calling from God to devote oneself to service in the church as a priest, a monk, or a nun. In the centuries after the Protestant Reformation, though, the term expanded to incorporate any form of needful service to fellow humanity. Vocation is now viewed almost entirely in secular terms. But seen as a moral choice of great consequence, one's vocation is still a "calling" to a life of service. What can be said about this choice? The following points may be especially important.

The primary criterion for a person's life work should not be the highest income. It would be foolish to ignore the importance of earning a livelihood, but to make that the primary criterion is to turn the "means" side of life into life's primary end. So the presumption should be *against* a vocational decision driven by money. A financially rewarding vocation can certainly meet the burden of proof, for the economic marketplace can also help us decide where our capabilities are most needed. But economics should be secondary to the main question: How can my life be most usefully spent in doing good?

Calling or career can be a hard decision to make, and having made it once doesn't ensure that we won't have to make it again, and again after that. It may have to be changed or remade as a person's life circumstances change. Obviously the choice will be unique to each of us. Not everybody should be a lawyer, or a plumber, or a doctor, or a minister, or a teacher, or a farmer, or an electrician, or any one of thousands of other possibilities. Paul's brilliant metaphor of the church as the body of Christ can well be employed for the wider society as well. We are all members of the great community, and each of us can contribute in our own way in cooperation with others who also pursue unique and different life courses. Perhaps the choice of calling can be put in this way: Our calling is at the intersection of our abilities and interests and the community's need. Those abilities and interests are partly inborn, but largely acquired and nurtured. In making the big decisions about a life's work, we can take into consideration the advice of parents, friends, and counselors of course, so long as we can trust that such advice is in harmony with our deepest values. Because decisions about one's career are developed in the context of educational opportunity, every young person's immediate calling is to devote himself or herself to being as good a student as possible. Young people should also try to pursue a diverse set of educational experiences, in order to be exposed to a broader range of possibilities for long-range vocational decision.

THE USES OF OUR MONEY

The way we use money requires us to make numerous moral choices. That does not mean that material consumption should be enshrouded by guilt, although for many people in our society overconsumption is a moral issue. Money represents the power to do good—both for ourselves and for others. I am reluctant to frame this as placing a presumption against any personal expenditure, but perhaps a presumption can be established for contributing a definable part of our material resources. The biblical concept of tithing—giving a tenth of one's income and wealth "to God"—represents what I'm talking about. Today we might say that 10 percent of one's income will be taken off the top for good purposes unrelated to our personal self-interest, and then make the burden of proof be borne by deviating from that standard. Persons who are wealthier should make the standard higher, and poor persons may have greater need for a larger consumption of their own resources. Any pastor is likely to tell you, however, that often the poorest people in a congregation give the highest proportion of their income to the institution. The story of Jesus pointing out the widow's mite illustrates the point biblically.

How should we use that 10 percent? For a person who is devoted to their church, that can well have the first claim, for the church most clearly reflects the purposes of life as that person understands them. But many other good causes and needs offer opportunities for us to engage creatively with purposes beyond ourselves: for example, United Way agencies, overseas relief programs, a particular person or family in need, human rights organizations—the list could be endless and beyond our capacity to give to all. But giving a portion of one's income regularly enables us to respond to such opportunities. If done regularly, it can become habit forming, and no longer a hard choice.

What about personal consumption, especially the overconsumption so many of us seem to engage in today? Setting an example of economic restraint makes a serious moral contribution to the community. Obviously a family's basic needs for food, clothing, shelter, medical care, and transportation must be taken care of, and so must its educational and recreational needs. As a general point, our standards of personal consumption should enable us to be an accepted participant in the life of our community. That does not mean competitive status seeking, or even "keeping up with the Joneses." There is, in fact, something to be said for deliberately leaving that kind of thing to the Joneses, who might be enabled to see it for the foolishness that it is.

In an era of heightened ecological consciousness, individual choices matter. One of the worst purchases my family and I ever made was a gas-guzzling station wagon back in the 1970s. It would not even have been built if we had not specially ordered it. In time, perhaps partly in guilt, we sold it. But that meant that somebody else was still using it. More recently, many people in the United States have bought large, fuel-inefficient sports utility vehicles (SUVs) when smaller, more energy-efficient vehicles would have served most of them quite as well. The net effect has been the more rapid consumption of fossil fuels. The decision to use public transportation—rail or urban rapid transit—as an alternative to automobiles is often more practical and morally more defensible. Such decisions also impact the environment in helpful ways. So we can frame another presumption in favor of personal consumption choices that are more responsible environmentally. The burden of proof might at times be met by alternatives that are less desirable environmentally, but we should meet the burden of proof as we make our choices. Such choices involve the way we heat, cool, and illuminate our houses, including using more energy-efficient lighting and devices like solar panels, as these become more efficient and available.

POLITICAL CHOICES

Important political choices are regularly made at the personal level. That is especially true in democratic settings, but to some extent even in more authoritarian settings. In a nation as large as the United States, individuals can easily conclude that their single vote will not matter. Yes, it may not matter much as a single vote, but added to those of like-minded fellow citizens, it can matter a lot. As I explain more fully in chapter 7, the state is society when it acts as a whole, and the actions taken by the state reflect a very large number of personal decisions. Those who choose not to participate at all are in effect acquiescing in whatever the state does. But what the state does can, and usually does, affect the lives of people for good or ill in profound ways. When we acquiesce through nonparticipation, we bear some moral responsibility for outcomes we could have helped prevent.

The plain and simple implication is that persons who are eligible to vote should have a moral presumption in favor of voting. There can be extenuating circumstances that meet the burden of proof, but they are relatively rare. I missed one presidential election myself; I was out of the country at the time and a voting citizen of a state that had no provision then for absentee voting by persons in my situation. Sometimes overriding physical reasons also meet the burden of proof. But the presumption of voting should still be there.

How should we vote? Different people will answer that in different ways, and that is a good thing. As a general proposition, we should of course vote so as to advance our fundamental values most effectively, knowing that we may well misjudge both leaders and issues. I recall, with only some amusement, the Maryland governor's election of 1966. By virtue of a three-way split in the party primary, an out-and-out racist received the Democratic nomination. Concerned Christians and Jews of both parties, appalled by his racial views, rallied around his Republican opponent, a little-known Baltimore County politician named Spiro Agnew. We now know that Agnew, who was elected governor and later vice president, had been corrupted by bribes and was to continue that behavior. In retrospect, those who supported him might still have concluded that he was preferable to the racist. This illustrates the difficulty of knowing for sure how an elected leader will turn out. Still, the presumption must be for the party or candidate who best exemplifies our deepest values.

That Maryland election also illustrates another point: we are not likely to be able to choose a flawless candidate or a perfect party, and we should not expect perfection. Usually, though, there is enough difference to make one choice seem preferable, and there should be a presumption in favor of voting for the preferable option among the live possibilities. Sometimes one might feel, as so many in Maryland did in 1966, that both of two options are unacceptable or, while acceptable, virtually indistinguishable. In such a case, some would support a third option that has no chance of winning but will still have some symbolic weight. I would place the burden of proof against this option, primarily because what the state actually does can matter so much. Sometimes that burden of proof can be met, however, especially if the symbolic votes can affect the subsequent behavior of the stronger parties or candidates and if it really does not matter much who wins in the particular election, that is, if the two candidates are very similar.

But personal political participation is not limited to voting. Actions such as contacting legislators to express views on important public-policy issues can have some influence. Political analysts estimate that one letter to a member of Congress is often assumed by the legislator to reflect the views of a hundred or so people. Those who participate as volunteers in a campaign multiply their political effect far beyond that of their one vote. And all of us can participate in organizations of like-minded citizens to exert collective influence upon public servants. Not very many people should or can devote most of their time to seeking to influence public-policy decisions. But when such decisions impact the lives of people near and far for good or ill, the choice to spend *some* time at this has real merit. Perhaps a presumption in favor of devoting a part of one's life to seeking to affect the course of history is akin to devoting some part of one's income to worthy causes beyond oneself.

Most of us fall victim at one time or another to subjective factors that get in the way of our efforts to think clearly about our political choices. These factors include group pressure and our own subjective self-interest. There is a fair amount of evidence that most voters look first to the pocketbook issues most affecting themselves. While cultural values can at times transcend economics,[26] economic issues are more likely to govern actual political behavior. In recent years many politicians have been visibly reluctant to speak of the need to raise taxes, and tax cutting has often been the most popular campaign issue and political strategy. This perspective can easily be rationalized on the grounds that government is too wasteful—and responsible stewardship of public resources is itself surely a moral imperative. But taxes are the most important resource for the achievement of public good, and to oppose tax increases as a matter of principle can be to obstruct that public good.

To counter this psychologically understandable tendency, we might consider having a kind of presumption *against* our own interest rather than for it. The burden of proof can be met, for example, where the purposes proposed are truly needed or where the involved citizen is a member of a neglected part of society in need of special attention. As a woman or member of a racial or ethnic minority group, for example, one might benefit from affirmative action policies, but that should not necessarily create a presumption against choosing to support such policies. The preferential claims of the poor and marginalized, which I referred to in chapter 5, often require public action. But such action cannot occur in the absence of support from political choices made by large numbers of persons. We turn now to the question this points to: What moral presumptions should guide us as we address the most important twenty-first-century decisions *collectively*?

7

Hard Choices in the Public Arena

In the United States at least, where vast numbers of people do not even vote, there appears to be a widespread bias among those who don't vote for living one's life entirely within the private sphere of family, friends, and very local organizations of one's choosing. This preference seems to reflect a cynicism about public leaders, and perhaps also a sense of one's own insignificance in our vast public landscape: "My one vote won't matter." But possibly it also reflects the bewilderment we all feel in the face of the ever-changing kaleidoscope of issues and dilemmas that bombard us. Some of these are perennial, even though they may appear with a new face. Some come to us as a result of hugely important technological developments. Some represent old frustrations; others present unanticipated new dilemmas. The moment we feel we have a grasp on the big problems, everything changes. It's easy to give up. But very few big problems simply go away. And the way they are addressed matters.

I cannot hope to resolve all of the big dilemmas in this chapter. Indeed, I may overlook your particular question or dilemma. My purpose is more modest: to suggest ways we can frame our discussion of the choices we face collectively, again making use of moral presumption and considering how and where we might place the burden of proof.

ABORTION

I begin with the issue of abortion, partly because it has so inflamed the American public debate since the Supreme Court decision in *Roe v. Wade* in 1973, but also because this issue helps illuminate the necessary distinction between personal moral choice and decisions taken in the public sphere. In *Roe v. Wade* the court held that during the first six months (the first two trimesters) of pregnancy it is a violation of the Constitution for a state to prohibit abortion, although it may regulate it in the interests of the woman's health. Only in the final three months may the government, in its interest in preserving life, prohibit the actual practice of abortion.

The court was unwilling to define prenatal life in the first six months as possessing that value the community must ascribe to persons; the definition of the value of embryonic life at this earlier stage is a matter for theological or philosophical decision, and thus beyond the proper reach of the law. The governing principle—the legal presumption—was a woman's right to privacy, that is, her right to noninterference with her freedom to choose. The court ruled that the state cannot enforce a value judgment that is in opposition to a woman's own value judgment. However, the court also held that the fetus, during the third trimester, can survive premature birth or surgical removal; on this ground, it ruled that during this trimester the state's interest in the preservation of life could establish a presumption against abortion. Even in the third trimester, however, an abortion must be permitted if it is necessary to protect the life or health of the mother.

This decision proved divisive. In subsequent cases the court has continued to affirm the *Roe v. Wade* decision in broad outline, rejecting most efforts by individual states to modify it. The debate has continued over the years since 1973 and at this writing shows no likelihood of being resolved. The nearest thing to a national political consensus may be President Bill Clinton's statement that abortion should be "safe, legal, and rare." But the debate as to whether it should be legal rages on.

Before further discussion, it is important to clarify the differing presumptions of the various participants and arguments in the debate. Those taking the "pro-life" position hold that prenatal life, at all stages, is the moral equivalent of life after birth and should similarly be protected by law. Some would treat this legal protection as a presumption that can be set aside for grave reasons, especially if continuation of the pregnancy is genuinely life-threatening to the woman, but others would not allow even that exception. Official Roman Catholic teaching, for example, holds that abortion should be prohibited in all cases. But by an application of the principle of double effect, Roman Catholic teaching says that the loss of prenatal life can be accepted if it is an *indirect* consequence of measures taken to save a woman's life. It is the *direct* killing of the embryonic life that is morally forbidden and should also be legally prohibited. (The principle of double effect is derived from the just-war principle that the killing of innocent civilians in war is permissible only when it is the unavoidable consequence of legitimate military operations against an enemy, and only when this "collateral damage" is proportionately less than the harm of not carrying out the operations.)

Those taking the "pro-choice" position do not advocate an increase in the number of abortions; indeed, a pro-choice person could be generally opposed to anybody's choosing to have an abortion as a *personal* choice. But pro-choice persons are opposed to laws *prohibiting* abortion. Some agree with the *Roe v. Wade* formula based upon trimesters; others oppose the outlawing of abortion at any stage. The pro-choice view is that making abortion a criminal offense is an improper government invasion of a woman's decision-making, thus clearly distinguishing between personal moral choice and public enforcement of the pro-life conception of morality. Their presumption is against legal prohibitions of abortion unless there are demonstrable reasons for it that are not dependent upon particular religious or philosophical views, or, to put it differently, unless a clear public interest is at stake. Is there such a clear public interest in the case of abortion? Pro-lifers insist that there is a clear public interest in the preservation of life. All of us might agree with this regarding the prohibition of infanticide, which is murder. But what about prenatal life? Does it, should it have the same status as life after birth, where we can speak of the newborn infant as a person? No doubt prenatal life is *potentially* a person, except in the tragic circumstances of severe abnormalities such as the rare instance of the lack of a brain. But is the fetus more than potentially a person? There are various ways to try to resolve the dilemma of "when life begins." One rationale is that the later in the developmental process, the more reason there is to speak of prenatal life as actually, rather than potentially, a person. At the very beginning, when embryonic life consists only of a few cells, it is more difficult to say that these cells are a person. From this the argument could be made that the longer the pregnancy lasts, the greater is the presumption that it should be protected. *Roe v. Wade* seems to have allowed for that by its provisions for the third trimester. Another proposal is to attach personhood to the development of particular organs—such as a beating heart or discernible brain waves. Those who consider cognitive capability to be what defines us as persons (as the various personalist schools of thought tend to do) could argue that rudimentary personhood exists when the prenatal being has developed some degree of consciousness—not necessarily self-consciousness, but at least awareness of the fetal environment. Admittedly, however, this is difficult to measure. I once put the question to the late Nobel scientist Joshua Lederberg. When, I asked him, could we say that a fetus has this capacity of consciousness? He surprised me by saying that the old Thomistic principle of "ensoulment" (when the soul enters the body) had something to be said for it, that point being when the woman experiences "quickening"—movement within the uterus, such as the fetus kicking. While Lederberg agreed that this does not resolve the problem with precision, in general he thought that this prenatal activity implied a central nervous system that was sufficiently integrated. And that rudimentary activity can be discerned roughly at the fifth or sixth month of pregnancy—again coinciding, more or less, with the *Roe v. Wade* formula. Following this line of reasoning, the state could legislate a presumption in favor of preserving life during that last trimester, while maintaining a presumption against interference at an earlier stage.

Still, any interference by the state with a woman's right to choose amounts to telling a woman that she is required, by criminal statute, to carry prenatal life within her own body that she no longer wishes to. It also interferes with the freedom of doctors to respond to what they consider to be the best interests of their female patients—with predictably chilling effects upon health care professionals and their hospitals and clinics.

The years of debate have produced other quandaries and dilemmas related to abortion: What are the rights and responsibilities of the parents of young adolescents who have become pregnant? Should the state require them to be notified? Perhaps a presumption should be that they be drawn into any decision involving abortion, bearing in mind that there can be compelling reasons in particular cases for keeping dysfunctional parents *out* of the process. And should the potential father be enabled by law to participate in the decision for or against an abortion? Ideally the potential father should be involved, but in the event of unreconcilable differences between the man and the woman, the presumption might well be that the potential mother should have the final say.

In respect to abortion—as in other areas where people may want to enlist the state to enforce their moral views—we should be reminded that when a largely unenforceable law is enacted, it sows both confusion and a climate of disrespect for all law. The many abortions conducted in the United States, often under medically hazardous conditions, prior to the Supreme Court decision in *Roe v. Wade*, suggest that a return to laws prohibiting abortion would largely be unenforceable.

HOMOSEXUALITY

Another highly inflamed public issue concerns whether the relationships of homosexual persons, often termed gay and lesbian, should be accepted publicly. Attitudes have been steadily evolving since the late 1960s, and the cultural acceptance and recognition of legal rights has grown. One important reason for this increasing tolerance is that more and more gay and lesbian persons have allowed themselves to be identified as gay by public acknowledgment or by themselves telling friends and family members. Since many gays and lesbians had long led lives that everyone perceived to be quite normal, this has helped allay the more traditional and long-held fears. Public debate has centered on such questions as whether committed same-gender unions should be recognized by law as marriages or, short of that, whether such unions should be recognized with all or most of the legal rights attached to marriage, but not called by that name. That these questions could even be debated is evidence of some cultural change—for gay or lesbian sexual relationships were until recent decades prohibited in criminal law codes and not considered fit for polite conversation. There now seems to be a national consensus, solidified by the courts, that homosexual relationships should not be illegal. Thus the personal choices of gay and lesbian persons remain their private responsibility.

There is far less agreement, however, on the issue of whether such relationships should have enhanced legal status. Gay and lesbian groups and their advocates seek this status in two ways. First, they seek the inclusion of crimes of passion against gay and lesbian people in federal laws against hate crimes. Second, they seek legal recognition and regulation of same-gender marriage or at least of committed unions not labeled as marriage but accorded similar legal protections.

Some of the opposition to such legal protections may derive from homophobia, if that term is taken to mean a strong emotional prejudice against gay and lesbian people. Homophobia is doubtless a reality, though increasingly those opposed to the legal recognition of gay and lesbian relationships disavow that label. People who are homophobic by disposition will, of course, place a strong presumption against such legal recognition. Some might be open to considerations that could meet a severe burden of proof, such as very clear evidence that homosexual orientation is acquired genetically or that people they know and admire have turned out to be gay or lesbian. But setting the highly subjective factor aside, opposition appears to be based on two things: The first is a belief that homosexual people are intrinsically promiscuous, and that society has an important interest in discouraging promiscuity. Such a judgment about the state's interest can be buttressed by religious beliefs equating promiscuity and idolatry and the idea that homosexual (or heterosexual) persons have made a god out of their sexual preferences and activities. It may be noteworthy here that the rise of the gay liberation movement in the 1970s corresponded to a period of widespread sexual looseness in American society, with "lifestyle" choices taken to be altogether personal and beyond moral evaluation. In many ways the culture has moved beyond this, for example, with premarital sexual relationships being largely monogamous in character. While the change must not be overstated, it is still likely that many people, especially older people, still associate homosexuality with the often blatant excesses of the period of the 1970s.

The second and perhaps more important reason for the opposition to homosexuality is the belief that a homosexual "lifestyle" is chosen, not given biologically. This belief fuels the fear that with enhanced legal recognition of homosexuality, many more young people will be attracted or even recruited to homosexual orientation and practice. Widely publicized instances of sexual predation upon young people, such as the scandalous behavior of a number of clergy and teachers, underscore the fear. Recognition of gay/lesbian groups in high schools and colleges, and the treatment of gay/lesbian relationships as normal in classes dealing with health and sexuality, are further cause for alarm among many.

With such cultural and psychological attitudes at work, how are the public policy issues to be framed? These issues too are hard moral choices and unavoidable, even though they are not identical with the choices facing individuals. If it could be proved that homosexual orientation and practice are both chosen and demonstrably damaging to individuals and society, there might be a basis for a presumption against the social approval and legal enablement of homosexual behavior, with space for the burden of proof to accommodate human weakness and other practicalities.

But in the twenty-first century neither of these conventional assumptions is holding up very well. Is homosexuality a choice? The near unanimous report of gay and lesbian people, now that it has become less dangerous to speak out, is that they have experienced this orientation as a "given" in their lives, not a decision on their part. Many describe it as a range of feelings they have had for as long as they can remember. Some ask why anyone would *choose* a sexual orientation that is so stigmatized and sometimes persecuted in our society. In response, some critics might argue that such a choice is precisely evidence of psychological disorder with socially dysfunctional consequences—which would, of course, depart from the theory that this is a matter of choice.

But is there evidence that homosexuality is a psychological disorder? Doubtless there are gay and lesbian people who are psychologically troubled; indeed, having to live with a stigmatized sexual orientation, often pretending to be heterosexual, could only exacerbate a person's existing psychological problems. Many therapists with experience in treating homosexual clients are concerned about that and are alarmed by the numbers of attempted and successful suicides among gay and lesbian young people who face conflict and frustration in their efforts to conform to society's norms and change their identities.

Despite these tragic experiences, it has nonetheless become increasingly clear that large numbers of gay and lesbian persons function quite normally, both personally and socially. Put in theological language, there are certainly gay and lesbian persons who exhibit all of the "gifts and graces" of their heterosexual counterparts. Theological language cannot, however, govern public policy unless it corresponds to clear secular purposes. In this case, the manifest normal citizenship of gay and lesbian people could reasonably argue for a presumption by the state to treat them in a normal way. To put this differently, there seems to be no good reason for the state to legislate disapproval.

What about "gay marriage" or same-gender unions? If custom and tradition create the working presumption, then the burden of proof is against formalizing such relationships through law. A higher level of presumption might well be the equality of all citizens before the law, but even if custom and tradition are to require a burden of proof before being set aside, it may be that that burden can be met. Why? Because if homosexual orientation is a given reality for most gay and lesbian people, rather than being chosen, society has a major stake in ensuring that gay and lesbian relationships are stable and not promiscuous. A gay or lesbian couple, supported by the legal provisions currently governing marriage, can together be a constructive presence in the community. Promiscuous lifestyles, made up of one-night stands and exploitative behaviors, are exactly the opposite of that stability.

Should gay and lesbian couples be permitted to adopt children? Many currently do, often with quite normal outcomes. There is no evidence, for instance, that the adopted children of gay and lesbian couples are any more likely to turn out as homosexual themselves than children in a more traditional family setting. The fact that many gay and lesbian couples *want* to adopt, is itself compelling evidence of the inherent stability of their unions. Perhaps we can come to recognize that, while sexual expression is certainly involved in same-gender unions, they are defined by love, mutual caring, and respect, more than by sex. That that is so can, at least, be the operating presumption in law.

THE DILEMMA OF "AFFIRMATIVE ACTION"

In the second half of the twentieth century, Americans finally woke up to the enormity of the injury that had historically been done to racial and ethnic minority groups and to women. Largely the gift of the civil rights movement, that recognition created a widely shared resolve to correct these injustices. The result was the acceptance of the idea that the rights of individuals must be respected, regardless of race or gender or any of the other labels that had long been borne as stigmas. So each person of voting age should be permitted to vote; all should have equal access to housing and other accommodations; everyone should be protected from hate-inspired violence; the state should, at all levels, be color- and gender-blind as it enforces equal rights. Now, early in the twenty-first century, these judgments have become so thoroughly embedded in the nation's moral consensus that even those who fought against them have been reduced to acceptance or at least silence.

But by the 1970s it also had become increasingly clear that simple protection of equal rights was not enough to overcome the legacies of racism and sexism. The continuing social effects of the centuries of injustice meant that it was not yet possible for large numbers of African Americans and women to participate fully as equals in American society. So the concept of affirmative action emerged, with deliberate policies to provide special, compensating advantages to previously oppressed people. These policies incorporated the idea that special efforts should be made to include more African Americans in university admissions, that women and African Americans should be given preference in hiring and promotion decisions in business and government—and in the nation's churches and other institutions. While usually rejecting the language of "quotas," advocates and decision-makers consciously sought to establish among their own members a visible presence of groups that had been previously excluded.

A strong moral case can be made for affirmative action. It is not enough to say that each person should simply be assured of equal opportunity in competition for a limited number of positions. The legacy of past injustices means that real equality of opportunity cannot be assured by simply removing barriers, for many people would have to start out too far behind. Moreover, the increased presence of previously denied groups in business, governmental, educational, and ecclesial settings helps demonstrate that the previous barriers were irrational and damaging to the health of the community.

The struggle continues today. On the one hand, a prima facie case can be made for color-blind, gender-blind policies throughout society, each person respected for his or her own qualities, irrespective of group identity. This concept could be treated as a compelling moral presumption. But the burden of proof for setting this prima facie view aside can often be, and often has been, met by the need to overcome past legacies of injustice, as we have noted.

But then another factor comes into play with its own issues: the perception that people are being given special opportunities for which they are not qualified. If that is actually the case, the next question is, have they been "accepted" as token participants, included only to meet legal requirements or for the sake of good public relations? If that is a widespread perception, does that call into question the qualifications of those who are, in fact, highly qualified? The claim is made that even highly qualified people will be put down as being where they are only because of their race or gender. Add to this the moral claims of a "majority group" (such as white males in American society) that has been denied certain opportunities solely because they are not members of a previously disadvantaged group. Is this "reverse racism" or "reverse sexism" at work? At what point can affirmative action be phased out? And how can policies take into account the normal human motivation to play the "race card" or the "gender card" when it is personally advantageous to do so?

These are legitimate questions, and they point to the painful reality of the continuing dilemmas that exist in public and institutional decision-making. But a very strong case can be made that, on the whole, the burden of proof continues to be met that affirmative action should not be set aside. African Americans continue to experience real discrimination (including racial profiling by police in too many locations); often their real qualifications and accomplishments are denigrated while the relative inadequacies of their white counterparts are over-looked or rewarded. Where African Americans have clearly excelled or demonstrated their competence on a large scale—such as in professional sports or the military—the need for affirmative action may be much less pressing today. In other areas, however, such as higher education, special attention can continue to help ensure the genuine inclusion of minority groups and women until society has finally overcome those tragic legacies of the past. Public policy and policy decisions in American institutions must continue to address the hard choices and social inequalities that exist in America today. But the dream of a society bonded together in mutual regard is increasingly shared by people of goodwill everywhere.

SECURING ECONOMIC JUSTICE

When Aristotle defined justice as rendering to each of us our due, he begged the question. What *is* "due" to each of us? Throughout the world, and certainly within the United States, this has emerged as a hard moral decision of great consequence.

The decision is quickly answered by latter-day followers of Adam Smith, whose libertarian theories support the idea that economic justice is best adjudicated by the free market. We are all free, they argue, to offer our labor in exchange for wages that we can then spend as we wish or to start businesses of our own, receiving whatever income our efforts and ingenuity can devise. Economic justice comes down to making the system work efficiently. The well-to-do may have a moral obligation to be charitable toward the poor, but that is a matter of their free choice and not a question of justice. Justice, in short, is render-ing to each what he or she deserves. That is the libertarian view.

Not surprisingly, those who hold this theory of justice are often quick to judge what they perceive to be the failings of the poor and even quicker to resist governmental interventions, regu-lations, or welfare programs. Much of this is ultimately derived from John Locke's theory of property, developed many years before Adam Smith's work. According to Locke, property is created by the act of mixing our labor with what we find in the state of nature. We clear the land of trees in the wilderness, and we have made a farm. We grow the crops, so they are ours to sell. We raise the cattle and sheep, so the meat, skin, milk, and so forth, are ours as well. We are clever enough to devise new inventions out of useless materials, so they are also ours, and so on. Exchange flows from this. We get what we deserve—no more, no less.

The problem is that even in Locke's time more than three centuries ago, there were immense difficulties with this theory. For instance, some of the land to be cleared in North America had first to be stolen from indigenous peoples for whom it was already their source of livelihood. Inventions were enabled by the largely unacknowledged cultural and educational developments that preceded them. Inheritance meant, and means, that entirely undeserving people are born to wealth. Social conditions enhance or diminish opportunity to participate in this grand scheme of justice through the free market.

Are there not even deeper theological problems? The definitive theological definition of property in the Hebraic-Christian tradition is contained in Psalm 24: "The earth is the LORD's and all that is in it, the world, and those who live in it." What are God's purposes for the world, and how does this affect our definition of justice? If, as we have said, God's purposes are best understood as an expression of love, then what is "due" to all is their well-being, as best it can be assured. Here my comments earlier about a presumption in favor of the weakest members of the community are in order.

In a 1986 pastoral letter, the Roman Catholic bishops of the United States had a different take on the issue of economic justice from the dominant libertarian themes then in the ascendancy. Economic justice, they declared, is defined by the inherent right of all to be participants in the life of the community. It is not enough for governments to secure such rights as freedom of speech and the power to vote; they must also do the best they can to assure the material preconditions for participation in the institutions of the community.

Consider the question of poverty. Over the past forty years, the number of people in the United States who live below the officially defined poverty line has been 35 to 40 million. The antipoverty programs of the 1960s and increases in Social Security benefits in the 1970s led to some improvement in these numbers, but the poor continue to be numbered in the tens of millions. It is estimated that on any given night 750,000 people are living on the streets, and 3.5 million people are in that condition at least part of the year. If economic justice means assuring the material conditions that enable one to be a participant in the life of the community, then the homeless obviously have not received justice. And the tens of millions of people who are officially classified as poor are short-changed as well: a poor individual or family may not be starving or freezing to death, but he or she is hardly able to participate in most community organizations. Sadly, the poor are looked down upon even in many churches. The costs of transportation and communication pose difficult problems, and even when fully employed, but at low wages, single parents and couples must often work more than one job. How can they be expected to participate in organized groups or to engage in mutual entertaining? Tragically, their children may be ridiculed or bullied by other children because their clothes aren't sufficiently up to date or because they cannot participate in sports and entertainment activities that cost more than their parents can afford.

The litany goes on. Barbara Ehrenreich's *Nickel and Dimed* [27] portrays with stark exactness what it means to have to live in entry-level jobs, even if one is fully employed. This enterprising writer set out to discover what it takes to live with entry-level minimum-wage jobs. Working in four different geographical settings as a waitress, cleaning lady, and Wal-Mart employee, she found she couldn't quite meet normal living expenses, even though she didn't have to use income from these jobs to pay for a car (she kept the one she already had) or for medical insurance (which she also maintained, using other resources). She discovered that many low-income people simply did without medical insurance, crowded together with others for housing, skimped on food, became vulnerable to accidents or illness, and suffered fatigue.

Some persons of goodwill deplore that these conditions exist, yet believe that they should be addressed by private charity and not by the state. But if we understand the state to be society acting as a whole, shouldn't the first business of the state be to enable society to exist in its wholeness? If society is broken, so that some are enabled to participate but others are not, is this not a first-order problem that the state simply *must* address? Otherwise, the society no longer exists as a whole, but only as a collection of isolated individuals. In one of his perceptive poems, T. S. Eliot raises the searching question whether we live together in the city only to make money from each other or to be a community. Surely the hard economic choices facing the state should be made in such a way as to enhance community.

The relevant presumption in the extreme circumstances of poverty and injustice should be equality, that is, society bending toward equality except when the burden of proof is met by necessary inequalities. In the United States that presumption of equality is largely met already by universal free education, and I will offer some further suggestions below. But are there socially necessary inequalities? Doubtless there are. Social policy, for example, must often employ incentives of one kind or another to motivate constructive behaviors and productive efforts. They can include special recognitions as well as economic benefits. Entrepreneurial risks, desirable for economic development, are accompanied by rewards for success—though often these are excessive. The engine of the marketplace does indeed seem to promote greater productivity, while pure socialism has failed to live up to ideological expectations. But productivity is simply a *means* to the end of human well-being in community; it is not an end in itself. At the beginning of the twenty-first century, the gap between rich and poor has widened, and the economic rewards for those in positions of corporate or industry power are seemingly without limit. To illustrate, by 2004 the ratio between corporate CEO pay and that of their ordinary workers had increased from 40:1 to around 400:1 in only twenty-five years.

CEO pay rose 15 percent in the year 2004 compared to 2.9 percent for average workers. These are broad estimates. Specific figures change from year to year. But the undeniable fact is that the gap between ordinary workers and corporate leaders has increased exponentially over the past quarter century.

So what steps might be taken to level the economic playing field? A more progressive tax policy would provide needed resources for measures that provide social and economic benefits equally for all. Some ordinary needs, such as health care, postsecondary education, and public transportation, should be assured for all, thus relieving lower-income people of some of their greatest economic anxieties. So people should no longer have to worry about health care and education for their children. It is in society's interest that all should be as healthy as possible and that young people should be empowered to be all that they can be (to borrow a military recruitment slogan, putting it to better use) through education. The economic playing field can be leveled further by raising minimum-wage levels to a point that allows wage earners to meet their family's needs.

What about welfare programs? The welfare reform legislation of 1996 may have been necessary, but it was a mixed blessing. Clearly the old program known as Aid to Families with Dependent Children (AFDC) was in disarray, and there was clearly a need for incentives for people to work who could work. But the legislation probably went too far. Not enough was done to ensure that jobs were available to all; simple trust in market forces to provide enough jobs and jobs at sufficient wage levels was largely misplaced. As a result, poverty rates were not much affected, even though welfare rolls were substantially reduced. The large philosophical (and theological) problem with the welfare reform was that it diminished the principle that society is responsible for ensuring the capacity of all to be participants. It is admittedly difficult to construct welfare programs that accommodate that need, but the task remains before us. When proposals are advanced for creating a negative income tax, enlarging the food-stamp program, or establishing suitable housing for the homeless, the burden of proof should be borne by those who oppose the ideas. The existence of poverty in America and the huge disparities of income between rich and poor mean that even imperfect programs can be an improvement over the present intolerable situation.

ENVIRONMENTAL POLICIES

All of us as individuals have moral responsibilities to help protect the environment for future generations. Our choices about things like personal consumption, travel, and heating and lighting our homes are morally important. But these personal choices are also intimately related to the collective decisions made in the public sphere. For instance, we cannot choose to use public transportation in urban settings if a good transit system does not exist. We will continue to use gas-guzzling vehicles if the gas they guzzle remains cheap. We will use fossil fuels excessively if alternative forms of energy are not available. Large-scale collective decisions must be made in order to enable responsible personal choices, rather than frustrate those choices. Enabling actions can be taken by corporations, of course, but market forces alone have been shown to be demonstrably inadequate. Public policies can help or hinder by regulating those market forces and by providing incentives.

Today, in the early years of the twenty-first century, the majority of scientists agree that huge increases in the use of fossil fuels over the past century have resulted in global warming. As a result of this global warming, we are faced in the coming decades with the rapid melting of polar ice caps, rising sea levels, the flooding of highly populated coastal areas, and climate change and its impact. The science on which the worst forecasts are based is controversial, but there is enough evidence of environmental risk to warrant concern by competent specialists. How are citizens and public-policy makers to respond? A strong case can be made that the presumptions guiding the development of public environmental policy should be to diminish our reliance on fossil fuels, to explore and develop alternative and less threatening sources of energy, and to facilitate responsible energy-related choices by individuals. An example of a public policy influencing individual choices is tax-related incentives for insulation and solar panels in homes.

Many of the environmental issues relate to transportation policies. The development and maintenance of the U.S. interstate highway system was a huge, very expensive public works project. The increase in air travel has had further negative effects on the environment, using vast quantities of aviation fuel and releasing pollutants in the atmosphere. We may not have to dismantle these systems, but they have obviously led to burgeoning uses of fossil fuels.

But cannot similar resources be devoted to practical alternatives? One of my earlier childhood memories is of the interurban trolley system linking my village in northern Ohio with nearby Toledo. I understand that such systems were abandoned in the 1930s and 1940s in favor of highways, automobiles, and buses. That abandonment may have been a huge mistake, whatever we may say about motor vehicles. Perhaps it is time to construct something like that to link localities, along with the development of high-speed rail transportation between cities, to diminish our reliance upon air travel.

Can we increase our use of nuclear energy in the United States? In some countries nuclear power plants generate significant amounts of energy (through conversion to electric power grids and thence to users). France, for example, is heavily dependent upon nuclear energy. The main advantage of nuclear energy is that it is not a pollutant. There are several disadvantages, however. The first and most serious is the possibility of nuclear accidents such as those at Three Mile Island in Pennsylvania in 1979 and at Chernobyl in Ukraine in 1986. While the Three Mile Island accident resulted in no reported injuries or deaths, it is estimated that between 80,000 and 120,000 persons died as a result of the large-scale release of radioactivity at Chernobyl. Ironically, the cause of Chernobyl was human error, as safety tests were being conducted too carelessly. But even if sufficient protections can be depended upon—as, on the whole, they probably can be—we face the monumental problem of disposal of radioactive wastes, which will have to be stored safely for an estimated 100,000 years. Perhaps, at this point of scientific understanding, the presumption should be against reliance upon nuclear power. A burden of proof could, of course, be met by technical developments that eliminated the current concerns.

Solar, wind, and geothermal developments play a minor role in energy policy today, but were social policy to change, so could their role. It is beyond my purpose here to lay out detailed alternatives to our present reliance upon fossil fuels or nuclear power. But the presumptions guiding public policy should be weighted heavily in favor of the alternatives.

CRIMINAL JUSTICE

Most human societies—certainly all large and diverse ones— have had to cope with antisocial behavior. Laws define crime, provide for enforcement, and specify punishments. Such laws vary from one country to another (and in the United States, from one state to another), but those three aspects of a criminal justice system—the definition of crime, the means of enforcement, and specific punishments—are universal. How should they be framed ethically?

A criminal justice system is largely negative in practice, even as it aims for positive results. No society can simply ignore social offenses, even though what is defined as an offense in one setting or time may not be in another. The manufacture and sale of alcoholic beverages was, for example, a criminal offense in the United States in the 1920s, but is not today. In some states where organized gambling was prohibited by law, it now proceeds with active state sponsorship. Debates rage over whether the sale of drugs like marijuana and cocaine should remain criminal offenses. There will doubtless continue to be social controversy over what kinds of behaviors should be defined as punishable crimes. While these debates are important, the larger issues facing the United States in the twenty-first century have to do with enforcement and penalties.

In respect to enforcement, the law should, and generally does, presume the innocence of all citizens, even though police, prosecutors, juries, and even judges sometimes fail to keep faith with that principle. In the United States a person accused of crime is presumed to be not guilty unless guilt can be proved beyond reasonable doubt. That presumption establishes a fundamental civil covenant of mutual trust and means, among other things, that people are not vulnerable to baseless accusation. This covenant extends beyond the rights of the accused and protects everyone against arbitrary searches and questionings without probable cause. In most cases, probable cause must be determined by a supposedly independent judge. The presumption of innocence means that even a person who has been arrested has the right to remain silent and to have access to an attorney.

Since September 11, 2001, and the subsequent presidential proclamation of a "war on terror," some of the fundamental protections established by the covenant of mutual trust have been hotly debated. The Bush administration sought, and largely gained, extended authority to wiretap communications in an effort to identify and deal with terrorist plots and conspiracies. The administration also found itself responsible for foreign detainees, such as suspected terrorists apprehended in Afghanistan, and sought to deal with them outside the regular judicial system—including incarceration not subjected to the right of habeas corpus and, contrary to commitments under the Geneva Conventions, the use of forms of physical coercion (such as waterboarding) that most reasonable observers considered to be torture. These prisoners also lacked normal access to attorneys and full rights to examine and respond to evidence against them, as in a normal judicial proceeding. Can such deviations from judicial protections be justified?

Setting aside the question whether they are even effective, exceptions to and deviations from legal precedent and policy must face a very high burden of proof. A foreign national under the control of U.S. authorities should be granted a presumption of innocence and a presumption against the use of procedures that are contrary to the U.S. Bill of Rights for three reasons. First, as fellow human beings they belong to the same universal moral community as American citizens. Second, as persons detained under U.S. authority, they have become *subjects* of this national community. And third, the U.S. treatment of foreign nationals sends a powerful message of respect or disrespect to people everywhere.

What moral constraints should govern the punishment of offenses? Crime and criminal behavior can create fear and insecurity in a community, and it is easy for a society to overreact to particular events and actions. In today's political climate, public leaders often feel they cannot allow themselves to appear soft on crime; and it becomes easier to support ever harsher penalties, longer prison terms, more executions. No doubt a society must penalize behaviors that it classifies as crime. But should there not be a presumption in favor of the least punishment consistent with the goal of social peace, preserving security, and maintaining a system of justice?

Bearing in mind that the correction of antisocial behavior must be positive as well as negative, there should be a presumption in favor of realistic programs for the rehabilitation of criminals and the restoration of the health of the community. This includes such obvious things as educational programs, psychological counseling, drug rehabilitation, and opportunities to earn limited income with hard work and good behavior while still in prison. Ecumenical religious programs of one kind or another can be helpful. Prisons are often the seedbeds of further crime, providing educational training for further criminal behavior. Are there, in fact, criminals who are so addicted to crime that they cannot be trusted to be a part of normal society ever again? Doubtless there are. No one would want a serial killer ever to be released from prison. Still, the presumption, thoroughly grounded in all of the great world religions, should be that most offenders can be redeemed. The task can be difficult, but it is also a creative challenge. That clearly is a primary responsibility of government, but nongovernmental organizations, including churches, have a role to play. Churches can be particularly helpful in ministering to those being released, in providing both a nonjudgmental fellowship into which those being released will be welcomed and practical assistance in helping them to secure housing and employment.

In the case of international war, prisoners do not have to be released. Nevertheless, as we noted above, under international law they must be accorded rights that are similar to habeas corpus protections. For example, the fact of their detention must be acknowledged (often through the International Red Cross), and they cannot be forced to reveal anything other than their name, rank, and serial number. Such protections are not only for the benefit of adversaries; they are also important in the protection of one's own military personnel when they are captured. (Largely for this reason, U.S. military leaders have been reluctant to endorse anything approaching torture.) William Tecumseh Sherman's dictum that war is hell was, if anything, an understatement. But the deep irrationalities of war and its savage inhumanities mean that a moral community must do everything it can to observe limits.

USES OF MILITARY POWER

The irrationalities and savage inhumanities of war mean that a moral community must avoid war altogether. That belief has been the enduring witness of Christian pacifists over the past two millennia, and their contribution has been to underscore the enormity of the evils of war. In contrast, those who are more influenced by the just-war tradition can acknowledge the weight of pacifist witness, while pointing to even greater evils that can in some exceptional circumstances be perpetuated by refusing to take military action. Would, for instance, military intervention in Rwanda have saved hundreds of thousands of lives there? Or would refraining from military action in Kosovo during the 1990s have cost even more lives there? Still, in the just-war tradition, the burden of proof falls on those in favor of the use of armed force. The military intervention by the United States and other nations in Afghanistan following the attacks of 9/11 might have met the burden of proof in just-war doctrine better than the invasion of Iraq in 2003. In the first case, it seemed more clearly a last-resort action, since Afghanistan continued to provide support and sanctuary to al-Qaeda following al-Qaeda's attack on the New York towers and the Pentagon in 2001. The attack on Iraq, which followed in 2003, hardly met even the traditional just-war criteria, and the grounds given by the administration for that invasion have almost all turned out to be unfounded factually.

But some of the most searching questions arising from just-war doctrine have to do with how a conflict is to be waged, and not simply with whether it is to be undertaken at all. Large-scale wars too easily get out of hand! The twentieth-century bombing of cities, for example, began with the relatively small-scale attack on the Spanish town of Guernica in 1937, immortalized in the famous Picasso painting. The world gasped in horror at this indiscriminate attack on a civilian population. But only a few years later, people had become inured to the bombing and leveling of great cities and the deaths of hundreds of thousands of people in London, Dresden, Berlin, Tokyo. By the time the first atomic bombs had been dropped on Hiroshima and Nagasaki in August 1945, the attacks were accepted and, among the Allied powers, even applauded.

Paul Ramsey argued that in the actual *conduct* of war there is no moral basis for this counter cities strategy. Just-war criteria specifically exclude such deliberate targeting of civilian populations. Harm to noncombatants can be justified only when it is the unintended but inevitable indirect effect of legitimate attacks upon the forces of the adversary. Counterforce measures can be accepted, he argued, but not countercities. Ramsey did not oppose the development and potential use of nuclear weapons, but he vigorously opposed their use against cities.

Even in accepting such limits, however, national policy making must confront some hard choices. What, for instance, is to be done if the adversary's forces (including missile launching sites and nuclear arsenals) are located within cities? How is one to deter attacks against one's own cities without being able to threaten retaliatory strikes against the adversary's cities?

Questions like these, in addition to posing real dilemmas, reinforce the conclusion that war has become a terrible instrument of national policy. Given modern-day military technologies, morally sensitive citizens and responsible decision-makers must insist upon elaborate safeguards and restraints, maintained with commitment long before the outbreak of any actual conflict. Moreover, the positive tasks of peaceful conflict resolution have become more urgent. Can a powerful nation such as the United States help foster a climate of international cooperation and peacemaking in which military decisions are less necessary at the national level?

The fact is that no nation, not even a superpower like the United States, can remain isolated from the wider global community. The world community does not have a political structure, with governmental institutions, comparable to a nation-state. But during the twentieth century it became increasingly possible to speak of moral decision-making at that level. And to this we now turn.

8

Hard Choices at the Global Level

Are there, indeed, choices to make at a global level? Does global decision-making even exist above the level of nation-states or lesser institutions? Should it? And if so, how might it involve ordinary citizens and political leaders?

INTERNATIONAL INSTITUTION BUILDING

Even before the beginning of the twentieth century, there were legal institutions of universal scope, including especially the Hague Tribunal, which was established in 1899 to arbitrate differences among nations. The devastations of the first and second world wars evoked much discussion of the need for an overarching authority dedicated to preserving the peace while also serving various international economic, health, and cultural interests. Following World War I, President Woodrow Wilson led the effort to construct a League of Nations, even though his own country failed to join it. During the 1920s international disarmament conferences resulted in agreements (although unfortunately they were largely disregarded after signing). The Geneva

Conventions were agreed to, by which nations committed themselves to certain humanitarian restraints in the conduct of war. Learning from the failures of the League of Nations, at the conclusion of World War II the victorious allies created the United Nations. And while the UN largely failed in its effort to provide collective security (mostly because of the subsequent fifty years of cold war), its technical, cultural, economic, and health-related agencies achieved some notable successes. Organizations like United World Federalists have nurtured the dream of a democratically structured world government, superseding what they consider to be the anarchy of the nation-state system.

How are we to evaluate, from a moral perspective, goals and prospects for programs that extend beyond our national borders or have a global agenda? Some aspects of the question are more easily dealt with than others. Take, for instance, the idea of a global government: Although huge concentrations of power always ought to be kept responsible, the rejection of a proposed world government on the basis of the belief there is a vast conspiracy to control the world and supplant freedoms with tyranny can probably be discounted as paranoid. And opposition to it that is rooted in idolatrous worship of one's own country is but an instance of the henotheism referred to in chapter 2. Most important, while we may, and perhaps should, love our country, the deeper moral perspective is that our worship should be focused upon the God who has created us and all that is.

But this answer is not sufficient, and other questions and dilemmas require examination. Specifically, where do we locate our basic presumptions in the case of global decision-making?

Twentieth-century Roman Catholic moral teaching has emphasized the doctrine of *subsidiarity*, which Pope Pius XI described this way:

> It is a fundamental principle of social philosophy, fixed and unchangeable, that one should not withdraw from individuals and commit to the community what they can accomplish by their own enterprise and industry. So, too, it is an injustice and at the same time a grave evil and a disturbance

of right order, to transfer to the larger and higher collectivity functions which can be performed and provided for by lesser and subordinate bodies.[28]

Subsidiarity seems to create a presumption for the freedom of individuals and small groups over against public authority, and it definitely establishes a presumption against functions being undertaken by a universal, global authority. The burden of proof to be met is that only the wider authority is capable of dealing with particular important problems. That was exactly the tack taken by the later Pope John XXIII, who wrote:

> Today the universal common good presents us with problems which are worldwide in their dimensions; problems, therefore, which cannot be solved except by a public authority with power, organization and means co-extensive with these problems, and with a world-wide sphere of activity. Consequently the moral order itself demands the establishment of some such general form of public authority.[29]

While this might seem to contradict Pius XI's earlier encyclical, it can also be taken as an application of the doctrine of subsidiarity. John XXIII is arguing that there are problems that cannot be dealt with in a satisfactory way by anything short of a worldwide authority.

But such a conclusion leaves many unanswered questions and dilemmas. How can a fully democratic and responsible international order be structured where so many of the component nation-states are not themselves democratic? How can people in small countries with weak governments be protected from the overreaching power of larger powers, even if the more powerful countries are internally democratic? Can one conceive of an international order in which large, powerful nations (such as the United States, China, India, Russia, and—if it can be described in national terms—the European Union) will subordinate their own interests to the wider common good? That may be difficult to achieve. Of course, the present international situation may reward the powerful even more than a more

universal public authority would. Still, the achievement of anything approaching world government seems well beyond the
reach of its advocates, at least for now. I am reminded of a comment made by a president of the UN's General Assembly some
fifty years ago. Asked about the prospects for the creation of
world government, this leader, who was from one of the smaller
countries, remarked that he didn't think humankind had suffered enough yet to accept that proposition. The world certainly
seems to have suffered enough over the past half century, but
the recurring and even increasing forces of ethnocentrism and
nationalism make anything smacking of world government
seem all the more elusive. History, however, moves in fits and
starts; changes, even very large changes, can happen unexpect-
edly. The great goal, transcending any particular institutional
form, is for the oneness of humankind to be felt and expressed
by people everywhere. That ideal can become the moral presumption guiding the particulars of institution building.

In the meantime, we can note that the United Nations and
its agencies have already accomplished many things. For
instance, the World Health Organization has had numerous
health-related successes, including the conquest of smallpox.
The Law of the Sea treaty has preserved the deep seabeds as the
common heritage of humankind. Technical standards have
preserved international air traffic from disasters. Even some
peacekeeping ventures have been successful, though that is
rarely the case when the project is opposed by major powers. It
may be that decision-making on the global level should proceed by addressing smaller and more particular problem areas,
rather than by engaging in ideological struggles. In that case,
forward movement may continue to be more incremental than
revolutionary.

INTERNATIONAL SECURITY AND POLICING

While most of the United Nations' accomplishments since its
founding in 1945 have been in dealing with the common prac-

tical concerns I note above, the original design for the UN called for a greater focus on collective security. The world had just been through the most terrible war in its history against one of the most demonic regimes known to humankind. The victorious allies were resolved that the world should never again have to face such evils and violence. The older League of Nations had failed to keep the peace; the new United Nations, it was argued, could do better. Peace and security were the primary objective, and the UN's Security Council would be the focal point for decision-making and action. The half century of cold war frustrated the primary goal, for the Security Council's five permanent members included both the United States and the Soviet Union, who were aligned against each other. Since permanent members could exercise veto power, no intervention by the UN could proceed if either the United States or the Soviet Union perceived it to be contrary to their individual national interests. This stalemate, ironically, made the world "safe" for numbers of "little" wars among and within the respective client states of the two superpowers.

The effective end of the cold war around 1990 fundamentally changed the situation, and collective action became possible, either by the UN or by regional alliances such as NATO. As a result, UN military actions were mounted in the Balkans, Kuwait, and West Africa that were at least partially successful in quelling interethnic violence and aggression. But the United States was unsuccessful it its efforts to secure broad international support for an invasion of Iraq in 2003, and when it invaded that country with a much smaller "coalition of the willing" nations, a quagmire resulted.

Neither Christians nor adherents of other religious traditions have the luxury of deciding policy for the entire world community. Still, they are, through their national communities, able to influence end results. Without exaggerating such influence, how should it be exerted? Clearly, the world faces very hard choices and dilemmas about the uses of international force. How should those questions be addressed by people of goodwill who are devoted to ideals of world community?

The basic ethical questions concerning international policing are not very different from those that make up the historic
debate between pacifists and supporters of just-war doctrine we
have already discussed, although the setting is dissimilar in one
important respect. It can be argued that no individual nation
has the moral authority to engage in international war except in
response to the invasion of its own territory or that of allies. The
international community could, however, be said to constitute
such a legitimate authority. This argument would not satisfy the
objections of pacifists, but it might address the concerns of
those supporting just-war doctrine. One of the key criteria of
just-war doctrine is that a war (translate: any military action)
must be properly declared by a legitimate authority. So the presumption remains *against* military action, but the burden of
proof can be met more satisfactorily by collective international
action than by any single nation. A peacekeeping presence by
military units under UN or regional international authority can
still more easily be supported if such units have not initiated
hostilities but only prevented others from starting them. In the
past, such peacekeeping operations have typically involved little
more than token forces, drawn from UN member states, without the capacity to engage in real combat. For example, a small
UN force has been deployed in the valley between the Golan
Heights and Syria for forty years. The force could not possibly
resist a major military operation by either Syria or Israel, but
were either to occur, it would potentially trigger more serious
actions by the UN as a whole. Implicitly, both sides appear to
appreciate and respect this token presence of the UN force.

But what about more substantial military actions that are
intended to settle disputes or to intervene in countries with terrible human rights abuses? Should the UN, for example, have
intervened to prevent the genocide of Hutus against Tutsis in
Rwanda in 1994? Was NATO right to use force to stop the ethnic cleansing of Kosovo by Serbians under Slobodan Milosevic?
Should Milosevic have been arrested and put on trial at the
international tribunal at The Hague for crimes against humanity? Should something have been done to stop the massacre of

thousands of people in Liberia by guerillas in 1990 and similar atrocities in Sierra Leone during that period? Should the world community have intervened in the 1970s to halt the slaughter of millions in the killing fields of Cambodia by the infamous Pol Pot regime?

The UN's fundamental presumption is against interventions in what are understood to be the internal affairs of particular nation-states. But these appalling situations suggest that such evil transcends national boundaries. Truly horrendous evils, such as those in Cambodia and Rwanda, cry out for *something* to be done! There is a growing international consensus in support of interventions, which can, I think, be supported by everyone who accepts the basic principles of just-war doctrine. The world clearly needs policing! But the "police force" cannot be any single nation or superpower that is ultimately accountable only to its own people and therefore likely to be attending mostly to its own interests. The United States, as the sole generally recognized superpower in the world, can scarcely regard its unilateral military interventions in other countries as a legitimate police action, unless it is done with a consensus of support from the United Nations or a responsible regional coalition of countries. So the moral presumption is against unilateral invasions by a single power.

While the presumption against any invasion of a sovereign nation, even by the United Nations, should hold, as several horrendous examples of human rights violations (and even genocide) remind us, a burden of proof can be met. The hard question is, where should we draw the line between legitimate and unacceptable interventions? Most of the traditional just-war criteria are adaptable here, including the question whether an intervention can be successful and whether it will be the course of least harm. Two traditional just-war principles may be especially adaptable to military interventions. One is the provision that a just war must be declared (that is, formally approved and initiated) by legitimate authority. This criterion can be satisfied by formal international consensus, for example by action of the United Nations.

The other, related provision specifies that a just war is a war undertaken in response to an act of aggression against a nation. How could that justify intervention in the nation itself? Would not the intervention itself be viewed as such an act of aggression? No, if the governing authority of the nation is itself clearly against the people of that nation or an identifiable segment of its population. In such a situation, the legitimacy of the government is called into question, for the situation resembles one in which the government has been imposed upon the people, who have suffered an aggression as if it were from outside. Thus the Jewish people of Nazi Germany and the territories occupied by the Third Reich were subject to the cruelest form of aggression. The Nazi dictatorship could not, by any stretch of imagination, have been understood to be their government. It was to them an outside force. In such a situation the wider international community could, by this adaptation of just-war doctrine, have intervened in behalf of the Jews. It is too bad that the world was so late in responding to that human rights catastrophe. I would offer the same judgment of the world's failure to intervene in Cambodia, Rwanda, Sierra Leone, and Liberia, among other more recent humanitarian disasters.

Similar judgments can as easily be made in situations in which a government deliberately allows a population to starve. Stalin's documented withholding of food supplies from millions in Ukraine and other parts of the USSR was just as lethal as the Holocaust in its human consequences and may have been on an even larger scale. Intervention in that situation, however, while hardly contemplated by the outside world, would have run afoul of other just-war criteria—especially the one specifying that there be a likelihood of success.

Sober judgment is called for in the many borderline cases of international aggression that take place today. There are at the present time many situations of human rights abuse where a case *could* be made for intervention. Perhaps even the UN should remain circumspect, reserving its resources and moral authority to clear instances, where many thousands of lives are at stake and timely intervention can make a large difference. If the UN and regional bodies are willing to assume greater responsibility for such policing, as I think they should, the world community can gain valuable experience in how best to cope with the worst situations.

At the present time, however, UN policing or military action depends upon the willingness of member states to contribute the necessary resources. From time to time proposals have been offered for the creation of a UN police force that would be specifically supported by and under the authority of the UN and not individual member states. Member states are reluctant to grant such authority, out of concern that it might be used against them. But would it not be in the interests of the world community and the cause of peace with justice for the world body to move in such a direction? The UN is currently festooned with and frequently burdened by checks and balances, and perhaps more need to be added if the world body is to venture further in the direction of world police force. But there is much to be said for it, as I believe global conflicts and the inability to resolve them have demonstrated.

NUCLEAR DISARMAMENT

The prefatory words of the 1968 UN Non-Proliferation of Nuclear Weapons treaty remind us of the grave perils of any nuclear war: "Considering the devastation that would be visited upon all mankind by a nuclear war and the consequent need to make every effort to avert the danger of such a war and to take measures to safeguard the security of peoples, (and) believing that the proliferation of nuclear weapons would seriously enhance the danger of nuclear war . . ." This is, if anything, understatement. All-out nuclear conflict would be a catastrophe of unimaginable dimensions, with probable loss of life from direct explosions and radioactive contamination reaching into the billions, along with the physical destruction of much of the earth. What would be left to the miserable survivors? The moral consequences of nuclear war for all humankind surely force two requirements: First, the steepest possible presumption should be against any use of these weapons. Second, there should be a serious presumption against further development or stockpiling of nuclear weapons and against the spread of such devices to nations not already possessing them. A similar presumption should be for universal nuclear disarmament.

Yet despite such flat-out judgments, dilemmas remain. First and obviously, even if it were possible to dismantle every single nuclear weapon on earth, the knowledge of how to construct them is now so widespread that there is no way that could be contained. The genie is out of the bottle, and has been for some sixty years. Second, there are already so many stockpiled nuclear devices that it would be extremely difficult to verify their *total* elimination. Given this, the handful of current nuclear states (particularly the United States and Russia) must maintain at least *some* nuclear weapons as a deterrent to their use by other, presumably less responsible, states. This deterrent may be, and probably is, regarded by some as a check against other kinds of hostile military actions, as well. For instance, during the cold war the U.S. nuclear arsenal was regarded by some as a deterrent to the invasion of western Europe by the huge conventional military forces of the Soviet Union. It may also have been a restraining force to some extent in the 1960s and 1970s during the conflict in southeast Asia, where neither the United States nor the USSR could afford to use the ultimate weapons. Currently more attention is focused on North Korea, perceived to have some nuclear weapons and missiles capable of reaching the West Coast of the United States. Widely seen as an irresponsible "rogue" state, North Korea, many believe, would use those capabilities as diplomatic blackmail. Could, for example, the existence of Seattle or San Francisco be at risk? Is that a compelling argument against unilateral nuclear disarmament by the major, presumably more responsible nuclear powers?

A 1986 pastoral letter by the United Methodist bishops illustrates this moral dilemma. Flatly declaring that a policy of deterrence cannot be reconciled with Christian faith, the bishops nevertheless did not advocate immediate unilateral nuclear disarmament by this country. They called, instead, for reciprocal, measured disarmament by the major powers—at that time, the United States and USSR. The bishops apparently believed that the continued, though diminishing possession of bombs by the United States would constitute a deterrence in this interim period, while also creating an incentive for others to follow suit. If there was some equivocation here on the bishops' part, we can consider that more charitably to illustrate a very real dilemma: On the one hand, the actual use of nuclear bombs is unthinkable. On the other hand, continued possession of the capacity to use them may deter others who are tempted to use them. Meanwhile, however, their continued possession by any of the present nuclear powers—and the likelihood of an expanding number of such countries—carries the ongoing risk of accidental explosions and irrational decisions.

Preaching on this subject on the fiftieth anniversary of the nuclear bombing of Hiroshima (Sunday, August 6, 1995), I commented that we can thank God that for the past fifty years decision-makers in the nuclear states had shown restraint in not using these awful weapons. The then-president of the United States, seated on the third pew back, nodded his head in vigorous affirmation. But I thought then, and do now, that we cannot forever count on such restraint, for decision-makers are also human, subject to human weakness and to extraordinary circumstances.

Is there a better way to address the deterrence dilemma?

To repeat, the strongest possible presumption must be against actual use of nuclear bombs and, I would argue, a clear presumption should be against maintaining a national stockpile of such awesome destructive power. Some argue that it would be possible to meet the burden of proof by the continued possession of a diminishing stockpile of nuclear weapons, concurrent with an equivalent phased reduction of such weapons by all other nuclear powers. I do not quite see it that way, however, given the risks of (1) accidental explosions and (2) the tendency among countries to want to join the nuclear club. These strike me as greater risks than the risk of the kind of blackmail I referred to above. (After all, if the fear is of a country like North Korea, the capacity of the United States to respond with conventional military might strikes me as a sufficient deterrence.) What is needed now is leadership from the United States, the world's leading nuclear power. Our government should at least clearly renounce any first-strike intention and refrain from enlarging or developing its present nuclear arsenal.

An even more constructive move would be to increase the authority of the United Nations, through agencies like the International Atomic Energy Agency, and to expand its supervisory functions to include safeguarding all nuclear stockpiles and helping to phase out all of them. I foresee much resistance to this suggestion from within the United States and perhaps a few of the other nuclear powers. But while the number of nuclear powers is (so far) limited, the risks of nuclear conflagration are shared by all. What happens to nuclear arsenals is everybody's business! The presumption, accompanying that fact, should be that decision-making authority over this awesome source of potential destructiveness must be universally shared.

ECONOMIC GLOBALIZATION

At the beginning of the twenty-first century, a huge international debate has erupted over the shape of global economic life. Decades of trade agreements, aimed at diminishing protective tariffs, have led to the formation of the World Trade Organization (WTO) and regional free trade agreements between nations, such as the North American Free Trade Agreement (NAFTA). These developments have encountered stiff resistance from activist groups and (often) from trade unions responding to the loss of jobs. But the movement toward the global integration of economic life seems inexorable. Insofar as conscious decision-making can respond to this process and bend its development toward good ends, how should the moral choices be framed?

Once more, we face dilemmas. Jobs have been lost in North America and Europe, as first-world workers have increasingly found themselves competing with developing-world workers, who work for far less money. Numerous companies have moved their production facilities to poor countries, where workers can be hired at much lower wages and with fewer protections—or none at all. Besides lowering the standard of living and employment opportunity of workers in developed countries, this has led to exploitation of workers in the poorer countries. Further, it has forced farmers in poorer countries to compete with farm produce from the United States and Canada that can be produced and sold more cheaply. This has, in turn, contributed to the large-scale migration of people from rural areas into the cities for jobs, leading to the creation of vast urban slums. Meanwhile, huge transnational corporations have the capacity to move production and capital around the world in search of ever more profitable ways to compete. A number of them possess economic power exceeding whole nations, and most of them are largely beyond the reach of national regulatory control. In fact, that's part of their strategy. A literature of protest against this version of free-trade globalization has developed, often with the implication that free trade is itself the problem and that countries should be encouraged to become more self-sufficient. Although documentation of the actual effects of free trade upon the developing countries is mixed, it is beyond dispute that people have been hurt. How should the international community respond?

Should there be a moral presumption against free trade? The answer is doubtless yes, if by free trade we mean absolutely unrestrained, unregulated trade. Many thoughtful people have long since concluded that a totally free market leads to monopolies, exploitation of workers, vast and socially destructive differences of income and wealth, and morally corrosive greed. Laissez-faire capitalism has failed to deliver on its libertarian promises. Most countries, to the extent they are able, seek to maintain regulatory controls. That is more difficult for individual countries confronting the economic power of great corporations.

Notwithstanding the real social and ethical problems of unregulated trade, a case can be made that trade itself is essential to economic well-being. That is true, whether it is on the scale of an immediate community, a large nation, or the whole world. Very few people can produce everything that they need—and it is much too late in history for everybody to be a subsistence farmer. There are far too many people, and far too little land. Even a subsistence farmer, capable of growing food and raw materials for clothing and shelter, must have implements made by others. And there are very few people who are willing to live at a merely subsistence level. I contemplate an advocate of purely local economic development arriving by airplane in a distant city to make the speech!

The United States, while dependent upon numbers of other countries for some raw materials, is one of the few countries on earth resource-rich enough to be largely independent. But consider a Bangladesh or a Chad or a Bolivia. Can any of those countries really go it alone? What are the resources each has to offer in exchange with other countries to enhance the standard of living of its people? Bangladesh, a populous country with few resources, has one obvious resource that is in demand in the world economy: cheap labor. And so, increasingly, clothing bears the label "Made in Bangladesh." That means they were manufactured in plants built in Bangladesh by international corporations that employed Bangladesh workers at very low wage rates. Ideally, this arrangement will allow Bangladesh to develop economically. The relevant question isn't whether Bangladesh workers should be employed at wage rates lower than those in Europe and North America. Wage rates will be cheap by world standards. The relevant question is, *how cheap?* Left alone, in the laissez-faire way, wages will leave workers deeply impoverished. Even comparatively high-minded companies will find themselves competing against corporations that cut still more corners. Some people doubtless benefit from this, including especially large numbers of Europeans and Americans. But, left alone, free trade is a devil's brew.

Where should the moral presumptions lie? Certainly not against free trade or globalization as such. Globalization, properly constituted, is probably the only way the desperately poor lowest billion of the world's people will be brought out of destitution and into world economic and social life. Foreign aid and idealistic efforts by nongovernmental organizations like Caritas, Church World Service, and UMCOR—valuable as they are—provide scarcely a cup of water in an ocean of need. People all over the world need to become *participants*, not just recipients of jots of charity.

But again, the haunting question, how low should wages be permitted to go in those countries where cheap labor is the countries' main point of entry into the world economy? Mechanisms exist through the international free trade associations, like the WTO and NAFTA, to regulate conditions of employment and environmental standards. But those mechanisms need to be perfected. The governing presumption should be that wages paid to workers making products for the world market should be adequate to sustain the basic health and well-being of a family. They can still be low enough to compete successfully in the world market; they must not be so low as to constitute wage slavery and continued destitution. The WTO, in cooperation with the International Labor Organization and member states, can perfect a regime that is strong enough to regulate even the largest corporations.

What, then, about workers in first-world settings whose employers have left town to set up shop abroad? That is a job for national regulation, supplemented by economic and social benefits to cushion the blow and enable people to sustain themselves at close to their old standard of living. That can include health, education, and unemployment benefits, coupled with serious public efforts to create new job opportunities. The presumption should be that these are public responsibilities, shared broadly by the whole community. Of course, the loss of numbers of jobs is—as free-traders argue plausibly—offset to some degree by the creation of new export-oriented businesses. But that is poor consolation to those who are not in a position to benefit from the new jobs thus created.

Globalization is here to stay, but it must be regulated more effectively, and this regulation must be done by national and international governmental authority. Nongovernmental social movements can play a major role as well. The U.S. market is especially coveted by international corporations, and when such corporations are found to be irresponsible in their labor and environmental practices, they may be vulnerable to well-organized boycotts of their products. An interesting illustration of this was the campaign of the United Farm Workers of Cesar Chavez in 1972 to unionize farm workers picking oranges for Sunkist Orange, a subsidiary of Coca-Cola. The threat of a worldwide boycott against Coca-Cola brought quick results. Another useful example of this is the Nestle boycott in the 1970s and '80s, which put pressure on that large corporation to cease irresponsible sales programs that induced third-world mothers to use infant formula products and undermined efforts to encourage breastfeeding, which is healthier and, clearly, cheaper.

Increased world trade, suitably regulated, may indeed be the most promising way to address poverty on the world scale. But we should not forget the smaller-scale improvements that can be generated locally. The Nobel Peace Prize, for example, was awarded Muhammad Yunus in recognition of his innovative and impressively successful work with microlending through his Grameen Bank.[30] This has helped focus international attention on how people in desperately poor situations (such as Yunus's own Bangladesh) can be enabled to develop small businesses and self-sufficiency through small-scale loans. His is not the kind of program that can be planned, top-down, by international agencies, but such programs do depend upon capital resources, and the World Bank can be helpful in drawing resources from member states. Small-scale enterprises can also be integrated with larger-scale industrial activities when the smaller enterprises are developed as suppliers for larger industries. Of course, it is also a priority to ensure that enterprises such as Yumus's, which begin with microlending to poor individuals, are protected from the exploitation resulting from overdependency upon supplying products for particular corporations. The subject is too large and complex for full consideration here, but it is a reminder that global economics continues to challenge local creativity and international oversight.

GLOBAL WARMING

One of the most serious challenges today is the prospect of runaway global warming, Scientific appraisals vary, but there is a developing scientific consensus that world temperature averages are rising at a level exceeding usual historical fluctuations, and that this trend may become irreversible. One danger is that the melting of polar ice caps, coupled with rising temperatures in the oceans, will raise sea levels enough to flood coastal plains in many of the world's most populous regions.

The international community has begun to take notice. In 1992, under auspices of the United Nations, a Framework Convention on Climate Change was adopted, which began the effort to control human activities leading to global warming. In 1997 nations participating in that convention adopted the Kyoto Protocol, which since then has framed the international debate on future action on the environment. The protocol specified targets for reduction of greenhouse gas levels, particularly challenging developed industrialized countries to meet the objectives. Compliance has been mixed; most notable has been the Bush administration's unresponsiveness and acknowledgment of the problem only late in its second term. This acknowledgment may have owed something to the growing scientific consensus, worldwide, that global warming is real, largely generated by human societies, and historically unprecedented. The UN's careful scientific work through the Intergovernmental Panel on Climate Change resulted in the panel's sharing the 2007 Nobel Peace Prize with former Vice President Al Gore, who was also recognized for his work in alerting the public to environmental problems. In a thorough review of the current scientific consensus in 2007, a working group of the UN panel observed that "global atmospheric concentrations of carbon dioxide, methane and nitrous oxide have increased markedly as a result of human activities since 1750 and now far exceed pre-industrial values determined from ice cores spanning many thousands of years. . . . The atmospheric concentration of carbon dioxide in 2005 exceeds by far the natural range over the last 650,000 years (180 to 300 parts per million) as determined from ice cores."[31] Most of this is from the use of fossil fuels. The UN panel avoids apocalyptic language, but the potential effects of these and related developments is cause for grave concern. Even with significant reductions in the use of fossil fuels, the atmospheric effects of prior levels of use will continue to increase for decades.

Uncertainties remain, both in assessing the dangers and in prescribing global policies to deal with them. Ethicist Peter Singer summarized the problem the world faces as it addresses the hard choices:

> How much of the change in climate has been produced by human activity, and how much can be explained by natural variation? The *Third Assessment Report* [of the UN panel] finds "new and stronger evidence that most of the warming observed over the last 50 years is attributable to human activities," and, more specifically, to greenhouse gas emissions. The report also finds it "very likely" that most of the rise in sea levels over the past century is due to global warming. Those of us who have no expertise in the scientific aspects of assessing climate change and its causes can scarcely disregard the views held by the overwhelming majority of those who do possess that expertise. They could be wrong—the great majority of scientists sometimes are—but in view of what is at stake, to rely on that possibility would be a risky strategy.[32]

The scientific burden of proof now rests heavily upon those who believe that global warming represents nothing more than a historically normal climatic fluctuation. We should be guided by a presumption that the scientific consensus is accurate and therefore that the well-being of many generations yet to come depends upon taking the danger seriously and acting upon it effectively. But how are we to do that?

The Kyoto Protocol created a kind of road map, with specific targets for reducing CO_2 emissions. Why have countries, especially the big industrialized societies like the United States, been slow to comply with its recommendations? The answer is simple: economics. Carbon dioxide emissions have been a result of the industrial development that created extraordinary prosperity in industrialized societies. Measures to reduce emissions, especially the sharp cutback in the use of fossil fuels, potentially threaten that prosperity. People in first-world countries like the United States are wedded to our automobiles, airplane travel, cheap electrical energy for increasing numbers of appliances and lighting, and so on. Following in our footprints are countries like China and India, whose economies are exploding and many of whose citizens are moving into the middle class and want everything we have—from cars to washing machines. Some people have little thought for the future and echo Robert Heilbroner's whimsical words: "What has posterity ever done for me?" There is a ready answer for that: Posterity alone carries the earthly meaning of our lives after we are gone! That is so, even if we find it difficult to love our grandchildren and subsequent descendants. The moral presumption must be, clearly and emphatically, for the well-being of those who come after us.

But this presumption cannot entirely guide us. What are we to say to the poorest countries that are striving to develop economically? Industrial development, upon which economic progress largely depends, takes a whole lot of energy! The rapid economic development of China and India in recent years is a harbinger of what will face the whole world in this century. China is already a major competitor in the struggle for the earth's limited fossil fuel resources. Do the Chinese have less right to automobiles than Americans, Europeans, or Japanese? If use of automobiles (and other energy-consuming machines and implements) throughout the world begins to parallel uses in the developed world, the specter of global warming today will become a nightmare in the future.

Guided by, first, the presumption that the scientific consensus is factually realistic and, second, the moral presumption that future generations have a compelling claim upon us, the international community needs to keep faith with the Kyoto Protocol process. That means placing significant international pressure on the more prosperous and energy-consuming countries to reduce or contain energy consumption, while finding ways to help the poorer countries in sustainable development. For countries like the United States, it also means exploiting alternative energy sources (such as wind power and solar heating) and adopting policies that sharply discourage use of SUVs and other gas-guzzling vehicles. New hybrid cars are a promising development. Public transportation, especially including urban rapid transit systems and high-speed interurban rail service, can be emphasized much more. Sharp increases in gasoline prices in the United States in 2008 had dramatic effects upon energy consumption in this country. This included increased uses of public transportation, an upturn in sales of small, energy-efficient cars, and a greatly reduced market for the gas-guzzling vehicles. This development seemed to lend credence to the theory that increased fuel prices is the best way to gain control overuse of fossil fuels in the affluent countries.

What about nuclear energy? It does not emit CO_2 and thereby contributes less to global warming, but it involves other substantial environmental problems. One of these is the risk of accidents—like the one at Chernobyl, Ukraine. Notwithstanding the pluses, a presumption should be against reliance upon nuclear energy, although serious exploration of ways to minimize the problems might well be pursued.

In this chapter I have sought to illustrate the hard choices facing the international community. Does such a "community" actually exist? Theologically it does, if we think of humankind as God's intended human family. Increasingly, it also exists at a practical level, as the interlocking forces of communication, transportation, and trade draw us all ever closer together. But the real work of community building remains a largely religious concern. People of faith everywhere face the challenge of translating their religious convictions into practice. For people of faith, that largely entails service in and through their churches and other communities of faith. In a final chapter, I wish to deal more directly with the hard choices we face in these institutional settings.

9

Hard Choices in Communities of Faith

In earlier chapters, we considered the deep basis of moral decision-making, emphasizing the importance of moral formation and tradition. In concluding this book, I wish to emphasize how communities of faith—such as Christian churches—can enhance our ability to make the hard choices and magnify our effectiveness in arenas of action.

These communities can be especially helpful in nurturing our moral consciousness—almost from the cradle to the grave. Here we are grasped by the meaning of love; here we are challenged to think of all people everywhere as our sisters and brothers; here we develop a deeper sense of history and how God can use our small efforts for a greater good. Here, ideally, we also learn the disciplines of civil disagreement and restrained conflict!

Anybody who has spent much time in an actual church or the faith community of any religion knows that our humanness often erodes the ideal. But churches can have a way of drawing us back to them over time. The early social gospel theologian Walter Rauschenbusch put it this way in his prayer for the church:

O God, we pray for thy Church, which is set today amid the perplexities of a changing order, and face to face with a great new task. We remember with love the nurture she gave to our spiritual life in its infancy, the tasks she set for our growing strength, the influence of the devoted hearts she gathers, the steadfast power for good she has exerted. When we compare her with all human institutions, we rejoice, for there is none like her. But when we judge her by the mind of her Master, we bow in pity and contrition. O Baptize her afresh in the life-giving spirit of Jesus! Grant her a new birth, though it be with the travail of repentance and humiliation. Bestow upon her a more imperious reponsive-ness to duty, a swifter compassion with suffering, and an utter loyalty to the will of God.[33]

The church can be an important school in the moral life. Possibly similar things can be said about great universities, although in the contemporary world many institutions of higher education seem more devoted to utilitarian missions.

Apart from nurturing people's moral sensitivity, churches are also communities in which the faithful take counsel together about the hard choices confronting them as individuals and as participants in the wider community. Often a church has within its membership persons who can contribute to this dialogue from different bases of experience and expertise. The resultant whole can be greater than the sum of its parts. A person with technical expertise can be challenged to confront the deeper questions of value, while the spiritually more sensitive one can be led to explore the factual realities that also frame a particular moral decision. All of us can be nudged to set aside culturally inherited biases that distort both our values and our perceptions of facts.

This can happen, to a greater or lesser extent, in almost any local church. It can happen even more in broader denominational bodies and in the ecumenical movement and interreligious dialogue. The twentieth-century ecumenical movement was especially productive when it analyzed the hard questions facing humanity worldwide. For example, the Oxford Conference of

Life and Work in 1937 represented a number of Protestant denominations during a time of world economic depression and ideological conflict. The conference offered both a careful analysis of the conflict between capitalism and Marxian communism and a profound critique of rising totalitarian political regimes in the Soviet Union, Germany, and Italy. The 1948 Amsterdam Assembly of the World Council of Churchs explored the meaning of a "responsible society," with its recognition of the intersecting forces of political authority and economic power and its affirmation of our ultimate responsibility to God. Other ecumenical conferences of this kind were convened regularly through the rest of the twentieth century and into the twenty-first. Not everybody pays attention to the pronouncements of such gatherings, of course. But people who studied the contributions of such conferences (with their preparatory materials) were nurtured in mind as well as in spirit.

Most of the issues I've discussed in this book would benefit from serious dialogue in local church and broader denominational and ecumenical settings; certainly the people involved in those conversations would benefit, as well. None of us is good enough or wise enough to go it alone, but each of us must not hesitate to make our contributions to the wider conversations. I have to admit that this book is terribly pretentious—except for the fact that I've written it in confidence that it is but one contribution to a great community of moral conversation!

What of the church in the twenty-first century, as it seeks to be relevant in new ways? I am particularly struck by the importance of the emerging interfaith dialogue. The adherents of any religious tradition have so much to learn from those of other faiths, particularly in sweeping aside old, unfounded prejudices. God is greater than any of us. If we are open to new insight, we may discover it in strange places!

Moral conversation within and beyond communities of faith can lead beyond insight to effective action. To be sure, churches and other religious bodies have made moral mistakes, sometimes doing great harm in the process. They have endorsed wrong-headed wars and attached cruel stereotypes to people they have not understood, forcing them to live stigma-tized lives in the midst of communities that ought to be more accepting. Even some causes perceived to be prophetic at the time have been short-sighted. In this category, I nominate the religious movement that led to the Prohibition amendment to the U.S. Constitution. Even though the movement's percep-tion of the damage done to individuals and families by alco-holism was morally sensitive, that perception was clouded by moralism and implemented by legalism. Quite apart from mis-placed prophetic impulses, churches have often been corrupted by their own materialism and greed.

But such flaws notwithstanding, religion has often been a force for good, in action as in thought. The great American civil rights movement almost certainly would not have been the suc-cess it was without the active engagement of Christians and Jews, first through the direct leadership of African American Christians, then with wider and wider participation by faith communities throughout the nation. Such actions contribute to greater insight as we face subsequent issues and choices. We learn from experience, not only our own but also the collective experience of communities of faith through time. In the end, as we seek to be faithful in confronting the hard choices, making our decisions, and living them out, we have to trust that some-how our small efforts will be blended together with the best that others can bring toward good ends beyond our imagining.

Appendix
Avoiding Pitfalls in Moral Argument

While the deeper intellectual resources Christians bring to their moral dialogues will always have theological grounding, we also need some guidance in our moral reasoning. In general, principles of moral reasoning are designed to help us say things more clearly and consistently. They spare us from saying more than we *can* say, or more than we want to say, or something different from what we thought we said. They can also spare us from saying less than we intend to say.

PRINCIPLES OF LOGIC FOR MORAL DISCOURSE

There are a few logical principles we do well to remember from time to time in our discussions of moral issues:

1. General moral principles or values apply across the board to particular cases that logically fall under them. There is a tendency in moral argument to settle things by appealing to one general principle. Often this will be an abstraction like "freedom" or "justice." When we appeal to such a principle, however, we should remember that we may not like some forms of freedom or some versions of justice. This leads to a second logical point:

2. When a moral principle or value is appealed to in settling one moral question, it may not be disregarded when it also applies to other questions. When I appeal to "freedom" as the reason for supporting a liberation movement in the third world, how am I going to react when somebody else appeals to "freedom" as a reason for opposing government regulation of private enterprise? If I oppose government interventions in the economy for the sake of "freedom," can I logically oppose freedom of choice on the question of abortion? We can all readily come up with illustrations of broad general principles being applied somewhat selectively. This does not mean we should abandon discussions based on general principles, but it does mean that we need to be a lot more careful in the way we see such principles. Rather than appealing to simple, one-word abstractions to settle arguments, we need to explain more fully what values we are appealing to and what their limitations are.

When Christians appeal to "love," for instance, we need to be aware of its multiple meanings, and we need to be prepared to deal with the question whether the real interests of love require negative things to be done. And when specific sources of moral authority are cited, we must not be surprised when those same sources become an embarrassment to us in respect to other questions. I have long had this principle in mind in my writing that we cannot use biblical proof texts selectively. Everybody tends to do it, but that does not make it logical. Liberals and conservatives both tend to use Bible verses when such can be found to support their case and to disregard Bible verses that are embarrassing to their views. This does not mean we should quit using the Bible. It does mean that the *way* we use the Bible in one context will commit us to use it the same way in other settings. I should not use a biblical proof text to settle an argument in my favor if I do not want other biblical proof texts to be used to settle an argument against my views on some other issue. The same thing can be said about the way we use science, or statistics, or anecdotes.

3. We must not, therefore, misuse our sources of data and moral norms. Sometimes we want to use whatever ammunition we can find in order to win an argument, quoting the Bible or science or statistics or anecdotes whenever they support our case and feeling free to disregard them when they do not. But this corrupts dialogue. When we use such authorities in this way, it often means that our *real* reasons for taking the position are quite different from the ones we are voicing. Sometimes there is a political agenda that has virtually nothing to do with the merits of the issue. We are more or less used to this in political rhetoric, where positions taken on public issues are often taken on the basis of whether particular partisan interests will be advanced or impeded—which is one reason why there is so much cynicism about public discourse in most countries. Obviously, within the church clear moral dialogue depends upon high standards of honesty. The purpose of dialogue is to help us all to discern the truth, not to defeat our opponents.

4. A single case is not a sufficient basis for broad generalization. We cannot say, for instance, that all poor people are lazy, just because somebody we met yesterday was both poor and lazy. Such a case may really be the exception. Much moral debate has to do with broad categories of people—racial groups, women, rich people, poor people, homosexuals, white males—as we struggle to understand the problems of justice in modern communities. We are all too prone to reach premature conclusions about people on the basis of insufficient information; we stereotype whole groups of people about whom we may know very little.

5. A single case may, however, be enough to challenge a *wrong* generalization. To use the same example, if it is said that all poor people are lazy, I only have to come up with the case of one industrious poor person to show that the generalization is not well founded. At least, those who offered such a generalization will have to change it to read that *most* poor people are lazy—but then we will have to ask for a lot more evidence. Fair-minded people are usually willing to acknowledge the exceptions. I happen to believe that most poor people are not lazy, but in fairness I must acknowledge that I have known some poor people who were! The very fact that a single exception is enough to destroy a generalization means that we have to make our generalizations more carefully if we expect to be taken seriously.

6. Not all opposing values or ideas are necessarily inconsistent with each other. Most of the foregoing logical principles are taken more or less from Aristotle's logic. But other philosophers, especially Hegel, have explored how apparently contradictory ideas can lead to a deeper understanding of truth that includes the truths of both sides.Much ideological debate has been wasted (and much blood spilled) in conflicts in which both sides were partly right. Take, for example, the Christian insight that persons are both individual and social by nature. Some contemporary ideological debates pit these two sides against each other as though they were mutually exclusive. For instance, the libertarians are exclusively committed to individual freedom, as though it were the sole principle of moral philosophy, and some forms of Marxism and fascism treat the social collective as the only important moral reality. But the Christian insight is that, far from being opposed to each other, the individual dimension and the social dimension are necessary to each other.

In moral argument it always pays to look at the apparently opposing views to see whether there may not be a higher, more inclusive truth to which both sides are pointing. If I may draw an illustration from some debates over feminism and the family, I have on occasion been struck by the tendency of some feminists to be suspicious of family values, sometimes treating the nuclear family as little more than an expression of the long-standing cultural subordination of women. At the same time, many who are deeply committed to family-centered values consider the feminist agenda to be a prime threat to these values.

But are the real concerns on both sides necessarily in conflict? Is it not true that a family in which women and men are genuinely equal is more supportive of the deepest family-centered values than a family in which men are dominant and women subordinate? And is it not true that women, as well as men, need the intimate, nurturing support of family life?

The point can also be illustrated in relation to our personal decisions. Sometimes our various responsibilities may appear to be in conflict when they really are not. Being a parent, for instance, is not necessarily in conflict with holding down a job and participating actively in community service. When people concentrate too exclusively on parenting, or their vocation, or voluntary service their lives are less likely to be whole and integrated. That may be especially evident when people do not take enough time for recreation. I have known pastors who did themselves, their families, and their churches a disservice by devoting their time exclusively to the work of the church. The different aspects of our lives may in fact be mutually reinforcing more than they are in conflict, provided we keep things in proportion.

I wish to pursue this discussion now, by highlighting several more or less typical traps to avoid when we engage in moral argument within the church.

TRAPS TO AVOID IN MORAL ARGUMENT

The straw-man trap

When we have strong views of our own, it is sometimes very difficult to be fair to contrary opinions. Sometimes we cut corners in argument by responding to the weakest part of those opposing opinions, rather than the strongest. Sometimes, even, we will restate the opposing view in an absurd form in order to demolish it more easily. For instance, if my "opponent" doesn't like my use of the Bible, I can portray his or her position as one that does not take the Bible seriously. If he or she believes in affirmative action for racial minorities, that can be portrayed as the view that racial quotas should be adopted regardless of individuals' qualifications. A mother wishing to devote all her time to parenting during the early years of her child's life can be portrayed as unliberated—just as a working mother can be portrayed as not caring about her children. A labor union seeking greater participation in company decisions can be portrayed as trying to take over. We can all think of illustrations, for the straw-man argument is a very tempting way to win a debate.

The problem is that issues cannot be settled that way. All of us bristle at having our views and our commitments misrepresented. Nobody's views seem very compelling if we suspect that they could not face serious examination. Therefore, it is always a good discipline in our moral discussions to try to state the opposing view in its *strongest*, not its weakest, form. I'm not sure I always do this myself, but I have always tried to teach my students in Christian ethics that they should strive to state an opposing position even better than those who hold it, before they go on to criticize it. If we observe this discipline, we will often find that we have something to learn from others. We will certainly find that they will be more likely to learn from us if they feel we are taking them and their ideas more seriously.

"Poisoning the wells"

"Poisoning the wells" is a colorful expression used by philosophers to describe one of the typical fallacies in logic. The fallacy is to stigmatize the one who presents an idea so we don't have to deal with the idea itself. If we put poison in the well, so to speak, we will contaminate all the water that comes out of the well.

I wish this were not done as often as I think it is. It can be a real temptation to dismiss everything somebody says because he or she has been labeled as a liberal or a conservative, a humanist or a fundamentalist. If it has already been decided that a certain kind of people cannot possibly be right, then all we need to do is attach that label to those whose ideas we want to see rejected.

The reason this is a fallacy is that good ideas can come out of people who have been dismissed in this way. One of the

tragedies of the McCarthy era in the United States is that the
contributions of many very creative people were neglected after
these people were smeared—most often inaccurately—as
Communist. If an idea could even be branded as "socialist," it
no longer had to be taken seriously—though most people did
not have a very clear conception of what the word "socialist"
means or of the contributions of socialists. Of course, the left
has also had its labels. We no longer need to listen to anyone
who can be written off as a racist, a sexist, an imperialist,
homophobic, or neoconservative.

The attitudes people hold do, of course, affect their ability
to contribute to truth. The views of a real racist, for instance,
cannot be expected to contribute to a better understanding of
other racial groups. It is also true that all of us allow ourselves
to be influenced by some kinds of people more than others,
because we are more confident of their basic value commitments. That will be true within the life of the church, where
some people generally carry more weight in discussions than
others. Nevertheless, the views expressed by all people need to
be taken seriously. Even if those views are entirely in error, it
will serve the dialogue to examine them patiently to show *why*.
We may discover along the way that most people have at least
something to contribute to our greater understanding.

These observations remind us of the respect Christians pay
to the humanity of even our bitterest adversaries. Our concern
is not only for the truth, but also for the person. Nobody is *simply* an adversary. How much truer that is of debates within the
church, where we are presumably engaging one another as a
part of the body of Christ. A very good discipline for any Christian congregation is for those members who have opposed one
another in debate most vigorously to make personal contact
immediately after the meeting is over. It helps remind us to keep
the issues and disagreement in proportion. Such a reinforcing of
the bonds of fellow humanity within the community of faith
helps us keep from falling into the trap of poisoning the wells
next time around.

The non-sequitur trap

The Latin term "non sequitur" is used by philosophers to speak of a certain kind of fallacy. In Latin the term literally means something that "does not follow." The fallacy occurs when we arrive at a conclusion without sufficient grounds. A crude illustration of this would be to say that everyone in this room is intelligent because they all have red hair. We may know that everybody in the room has red hair, and we may suspect that everybody is intelligent. But the fact that everyone has red hair does not prove that they are intelligent. Does this kind of fallacy ever occur in moral arguments?

Some years ago in the midst of the Vietnam War, a prominent lay theologian made many speeches around the country in which he denounced American war policy. Fond of shocking his audiences, he used to exclaim, "The Vietnam War is wrong because of the Resurrection." Without further elaboration, that is not enough. A connection could possibly be made between the theological implications of resurrection faith and the moral value questions raised by the war. But he had not made those connections. He had simply asserted a relationship. He possibly could have argued that the resurrection represents the triumph of suffering love and that rather than trusting in God's love, the war policy was a crude attempt to manipulate history with blunt instruments of force. But then he would have had to say more about the facts involved, and he would have had to say whether it is ever right, on the basis of the resurrection, to act forcibly in the world. He might have noticed that others could take the view that the Vietnam War was *right* because of the resurrection's implications concerning freedom from oppression. They too would have had to spell this out more carefully.

In all of our personal and corporate moral judgments, we need to beware of the temptation to leap too quickly from a compelling biblical or theological insight to a conclusion that may or may not logically follow. Stewardship is an enduring Christian moral responsibility, and that entails giving as well as wise spending. But not everything we give to—even in the life of the church—is necessarily good stewardship. Vocation is also a compelling Christian doctrine, but being called does not necessarily mean we are called to be missionaries or ordained clergy. Thinking together in the life of the church can be very important in helping all of us draw the right conclusions about our responsibilities.

The law = morality trap

When outraged by blatant immoralities or social offenses, Americans are prone to say, "There oughta be a law against that." In any healthy society there is bound to be a fairly close two-way connection between law and morality. The law reflects underlying moral values of the community, and moral behavior is guided by the law. Nevertheless, it is a common mistake to treat the two as though they were necessarily the same.

On the one hand, the law is not a sufficient standard for moral behavior. Many things are legal without being moral. It is, within certain limits, quite legal to speak in a cruel way to fellow human beings, but that does not come up to the moral standard of 1 Corinthians 13: "Love is patient; love is kind." It may be legally possible to sue somebody on a pure technicality—when they are financially strapped, we are well off, and no real injury has been done. But that could also be an offense to Christian conscience. From a Christian standpoint, a discussion of moral issues that goes no further than the legally permissible has not yet gotten off the ground.

On the other hand, the fact that something does not meet the Christian standard for morality does not necessarily mean that Christians should attempt to pass laws against it. Many people, myself among them, think it was a mistake for churches to force the absolutist position on alcohol upon the nation through Prohibition. Contemporary Christians who wish to ban all abortions through law should think twice whether such legislation is wise in a deeply divided community. In any event, the question whether something is moral or not is not to be treated as though it were entirely the same question as whether it should be lawful.

Premature consensus

There is also a certain tendency to reach for agreement before all of the differences have been examined sufficiently. This is partly because we mistakenly feel that disagreement is unloving or destructive, when the really destructive thing is more likely to be disagreement that is suppressed and not allowed to be expressed. There is a certain wisdom in the old Quaker tradition of waiting for the sense of the meeting. Some Quakers, no doubt, have always had more influence in the gathered meeting than others. But it was understood that no consensus really expressed the Spirit until it was genuinely shared by all members.

United Methodists don't go that far. We discuss things, but we also take votes. A majority can carry the day in adopting a resolution or agreeing upon a policy. Nevertheless, pushing for decision before an issue has really been worked through can be a trap that will undermine the group's integrity in dialogue.

The paralysis of analysis

The opposite danger is continuing to discuss questions long after most people have arrived at settled conclusions. Continued analysis may become a substitute for committed action. Most local congregations are surrounded by serious human needs to which they need to respond. Those needs should be studied and discussed thoroughly as the church reflects upon its mission. But there comes a time when it must get on with the task. I believe that a congregation must be a center for vital dialogue on important issues, but the dialogue itself is not likely to continue to be vital if it is not connected with actual mission. Perhaps the church is located in a city that has a serious drug problem. That is an important topic for sustained study and moral dialogue. But the study and dialogue will become empty if the church isn't also trying to do something about the problem. Dialogue does not have to lead to the paralysis trap, but we must remain alert to the danger.

The "ritual function"

One reason that discussion can be a substitute for action was explored helpfully by the sociologist Robert Merton. Merton's fascinating insight is that sometimes particular programs or practices serve what he called the "ritual function." When confronted by an unresolvable value conflict, we may deal seriously with one set of values or goals while "ritualizing" the other. For instance, a student who wants to study but who also wants to watch a football game on television may watch the game with a textbook in hand. It is likely that the book won't get read, but a gesture has been made in that direction. If we find that solving a social problem realistically will require more time and money than we want to spend, we may use our resources elsewhere while continuing to *study* the social problem!

Politicians are sometimes adept at this. Dealing realistically with health-care issues or poverty issues or criminal-justice issues may require raising taxes or changing budgetary priorities that, for political reasons, the politician feels he or she must not do. But a further study or a rousing speech or even the introduction of legislation with no chance of passing can be a way of *appearing* to deal with the problems. The ritual has replaced a serious, realistic effort to achieve the goal.

The church, as Merton's very choice of the word "ritual" suggests, can so easily fall into such a trap! It can pray about problems, study problems, discuss problems, and take up small collections to fund totally inadequate solutions to problems, helping to create for its members and others the illusion that it has done something important. I do not wish to be cynical about this. Prayer, study, discussion, and offerings can be important contributions to addressing problems. Even when they are totally inadequate, they can sometimes raise the consciousness of people and lead to effective action. Still, moral dialogue within the church will be more authentic when we anticipate the ritualizing trap and avoid it.

Creative moral dialogue is not, of course, simply a matter of avoiding traps and logical fallacies. I have emphasized the pitfalls here because these are some of the points at which genuine dialogue can break down.

Faced with troubling quandaries about personal moral decisions, Christians need the benefit of solid, logical thinking that is soundly rooted in the gospel. None of us is good enough or wise enough to go it alone. We need the challenge and the collective wisdom of the whole community of faith. And if this is true of our personal decisions, it may be all the more true of our collective responsibilities in the wider society.

Notes

1. J. Philip Wogaman, *Christian Moral Judgment* (Louisville, KY: Westminster/John Knox Press, 1989).

2. John Courtney Murray, S.J., *We Hold These Truths: Catholic Reflections on the American Proposition* (New York: Sheed & Ward, 1961).

3. In his essay "On a Supposed Right to Tell Lies from Benevolent Motives" (1797), Kant reinforced his conviction that there can be no exception to the rule that lying is *always* morally wrong.

4. News accounts and conversations with Liberian exchange students at the time provided accounts of this dreadful situation. For example, hundreds of Liberians who had sought refuge in a church in Monrovia were mercilessly slain.

5. Robert K. Merton, *Social Theory and Social Structure*, 3rd ed., rev. (Glencoe, IL: The Free Press, 1957).

6. John Rawls, *A Theory of Justice* (Cambridge: Harvard Univ. Press, 1971), esp. 14–15. The influential book has appeared in subsequent editions containing further refinements of his theory. See also his *Political Liberalism* (New York: Columbia Univ. Press, 1993, 1996), esp. 304–10.

7. Peter Singer has also criticized Rawls's theory of justice for neglecting its global implications. That may not lead to rejection of the theory itself, but it is a reminder that an adequate account of justice cannot be limited by national boundaries. See Singer, *One World: The Ethics of Globalization* (New Haven, CT: Yale Univ. Press, 2002, 2004).

8. H. Richard Niebuhr, *Radical Monotheism and Western Culture* (Louisville, KY: Westminster/John Knox Press, 1993 [1960])

9. Charles Colson, *Against the Night: Living in the New Dark Ages* (Minneapolis: Grason, 1989), 41–43.

10. © Barna Research Group, 2001. The research showed that among "born again" teenagers, 76 percent responded with the "Depends on the situation" answer!

11. Bertrand Russell, "A Free Man's Worship," in *Mysticism and Logic* (London: George Allen & Unwin, 1917 [1903]).

12. G. E. Moore, *Principia Ethica* (Cambridge: Cambridge Univ. Press, 1903), Section 10.

13. His presentation was based on his essay "Lifeboat Ethics: The Case against Helping the Poor" (*Psychology Today*, Sept. 1974).

14. Joseph Fletcher, *Situation Ethics* (Philadelphia: Westminster Press, 1966).

15. Paul Ramsey, *Deeds and Rules in Christian Ethics* (New York: Scribner's, 1967).

16. The importance of love as motivation for individual acts is also illustrated by the situation ethics of Joseph Fletcher. Rule agapism is derived from similar but nontheological insights from philosophers such as William Frankena and John Rawls.

17. Wogaman, *Christian Moral Judgment*.

18. *The Church Studies Homosexuality* (Nashville: United Methodist Publishing House, 1994), 36.

19. See Desmond Tutu, *No Future without Forgiveness* (New York: Doubleday, 1999), for a firsthand account of this remarkable story.

20. Reinhold Niebuhr, *The Nature and Destiny of Man* (Louisville, KY: Westminster John Knox Press, 1996 [1941]), 1:178–79.

21. Reinhold Niebuhr, *The Children of Light and the Children of Darkness* (New York: Scribner's, 1944), xiii.

22. John Bartlow Martin, *The Deep South Says NEVER* (New York: Ballantine Books, 1957).

23. *Book of Discipline 2004*, 100.

24. I still count it as my very worst pastoral decision, back in 1958, to have refused to marry, or at least offer sensitive counsel to, a couple because one of them had been divorced.

25. Margaret A. Farley, *Just Love: A Framework for Christian Sexual Ethics* (New York and London: Continuum, 2006), 305.

26. Obvious illustrations of this include both sides in the struggle over abortion and the often intense voting behavior of members of the National Rifle Association. As a matter of political fact, any values held passionately by voters can affect their electoral choices.

27. Barbara Ehrenreich, *Nickel and Dimed: On (Not) Getting By in America* (New York: Henry Holt & Co., 2001).

28. *Quadragesimo Anno* (1931), Paragraph 79.

29. *Pacem in Terris* (1963), Paragraph 137.

30. Dr. Yunus relates the story of this innovative development in *Banker to the Poor: Micro-lending and the Battle against World Poverty* (New York: Public Affairs, 2007 [1997]).

31. Intergovernmental Panel on Climate Change, "Climate Change 2007: The Physical Science Basis" (Geneva: IPCC Secretariat, 2007), 2.

32. Singer, *One World*, 16. See note 7.

33. Walter Rauschenbusch, *Prayers of the Social Awakening* (Boston: Pilgrim Press, 1910), 119.

Index

abortion, 6–7, 26, 87–89, 102–5, 158
absolute, God as, 33–35
absolutism, 27, 28
abstraction, appeal to, in moral discourse, 150–52
act agapism, 44
action, difficulty of assessing, xiv–xv
adoption, by gay and lesbian couples, 109
affirmative action, 67–69, 100, 109–12
Against the Night (Colson), 27
Aid to Families with Dependent Children, 63, 116–17
alcohol use, 26
alternative energy sources, 144
Amsterdam Assembly of the World Council of Churchs, 148
apartheid, 5
Aquinas, Thomas. *See* Thomas Aquinas
Aristotle, 30, 65, 74, 112, 153
Augustine, Saint, 49, 84
authorities, guidance from, 52–53, 71

Bangladesh, 138
behavioral sciences, ethics taking account of, 38–39
Bible
  authority of, 41, 79
  using proof texts from, 151–52
biblical commandments, responding to, 58–59

biblical theology, using as starting point, 58–59
big bang theory, 17–18
Bonhoeffer, Dietrich, 61
Brightman, Edgar S., 43
burden of proof, 47–48
Burundi, xiv
Bush administration, 54, 120, 141
business ethics, 43

Cambodia, 131, 132
candidates, support of, 10–11
carbon dioxide emissions, 142
Caritas, 139
Casti Connubii (Pius XI), 87
categorical imperative, 31–32
certainty, craving for, 28
certitude, 34
change, basis for decision to, 36–38
character, defined by moral virtues, 21
cheap grace, 61
cheating, 4–5
Chernobyl, nuclear accident at, 118
child neglect, 3–4
children, providing for, 3–4
Christian character, virtues constituting, 22
Christian ethics, God as absolute for, 34
Christian moral presumptions, 57
Christian pacifist tradition, 8
Christian Reconstructionist movement, 28

167